I0458978

Breaking the Silence

A Personal Journey of Healing, Resilience, and Finding Hope After Trauma

Dalia Abdulfatah

AUTHORITY
PUBLISHING

ISBN (Paperback): 978-1-965480-12-0

ISBN (eBook): 978-1-965480-13-7

Published by: Authority Publishing

www.authority-publishing.com

Printed in the United States of America.

To Yasser. I love you

To my family and friends who share with me the love of Talal

To my children who never got to meet him

To my husband, who has been there for me since day one

To Talal the angel who left us too soon.

Contents

Prologue

"Grief is not the enemy. It is a
bridge—a bridge between love and
loss, between what was and what
remains."

When I think about Talal, I see laughter resonating in cozy homes, peaceful talks beneath the starry sky, and a grin that might calm even the worst days. He was not only family but also a consistent lighthouse in a world too frequently veiled in doubt in my life.

When it happens, though, loss does not just take away a person. It grabs hopes, memories, and futures. Talal's disappearance left a gulf in me that I had no way over.

I pushed back against loss for years. I locked it up, believing it would fade into stillness if I ignored it long enough. But loss waits; it never fades. It waits in the silent corners of our souls, in the shadows of joyful events, and in the places where love once bloomed.

I am using this book as my bridge. It pays tribute to Talal's life, speaks for the love we experienced, and extends a helping hand to anyone else poised on the brink of loss. Though terrible, it teaches us that loss can also be a portal to healing, connection, and a closer knowledge of love.

I encourage you to stroll with me across this bridge as you turn these pages. Working together, we may investigate the areas where grief and love collide and find the brightness still shining on the other side.

Introduction

Grief can come into your life out of the blue when you least expect it and refuse to leave. It doesn't knock; it just walks right in and flips everything you know on its head. My story is the same. It's a story about love, loss, and the tricky path to peace in the middle of chaos.

When Talal left, it felt like the ground had been pulled out from under me. Talal was my uncle, best friend, and someone I could talk to about anything. We were connected in a way that was different from most relationships. His smile could make even the worst days better, and the way he treated everyone made an impression that would last. He was gone, though, in the blink of an eye, and nothing could have prepared me for how empty my life felt without him.

In the beginning, my sadness seemed impossible to handle. There were times when I didn't believe anything, and the pain was too much to handle. But this isn't a sad story; it's a story about getting better. In loss, I found life again, even though it seemed impossible at the time.

The journey wasn't a straight line. There were problems, nights when I couldn't sleep, and lots of questions. But the power of my family, the memories we had with Talal, and the love that never died helped me get through it all.

I've always been interested in health, even when I was young. When I was only 14, I stayed with a mother during labor at the hospital where my grandfather worked and gave her words of support. That's where I first found my love for caring for others and my desire to make their lives easier. These early events set me on the path to becoming a nurse, a job that taught me more about strength, compassion, and the human spirit.

As I walked the halls of my grandfather's hospital, I learned a lot about trust and kindness. When I was 15, I was put in charge of treating a child's wound. Even though I was young, people had a lot of faith in me. Over the years, these events have made me the caring and healing person I am today. I bring these traits into my personal and professional life.

Writing this book helped me make sense of everything and put my broken heart back together. I hope that these pages can comfort, understand, and maybe even give hope to others who have lost someone.

Even though grief may never go away, it doesn't have to make us who we are. Life can be beautiful again after a loss, even if it doesn't look how we thought it would.

The Day it All Started
The Moment That Shattered Our World

We were all gathered at Aunt May's house for the Sahur Dinner, a meal Muslims eat before fasting during *Ramadan*. Iftar is the evening meal to break the fast. Aunt May's home was like a scene from a fairy tale, with a beautiful garden adorned with twinkling fairy lights that danced in the evening breeze. The inviting aroma of Saudi coffee and delicious food filled the October night air, adding to the enchantment of the scene.

When I was 21, I brought my best friends, Deema and Najla, to this warm and funny get-together. My brother Yasser, Fareed, and some other friends joined us. Also, there was Aunt Dina, her family, and some other cousins. We dressed in traditional Saudi clothes called *jalabiyas*, which gave the event a lively cultural touch.

The house was built with many places to sit. In the big area by the pool, guests could unwind, or they could go downstairs to a quiet garden area in front of the basement. I was with some friends in one of these calm areas, where shishas and the smell of Saudi coffee made us feel at ease.

Traditional Arabic chairs were set up next to the pool to greet guests. The soft glow from the lanterns and candles hanging from the trees made the atmosphere even cozier.

Aunt May's meticulously arranged table was a feast for the senses—steaming pots of tea, fragrant coffee, and plump, glistening dates awaited us. Every detail, from the table settings to the carefully curated décor, reflected her passion for hospitality. With her welcoming smile, she guided us to the garden.

"Come, come! Make yourselves at home," she said warmly, her happiness evident in her sparkling eyes.

• • • ● • ● • • •

My younger brother Yasser wasn't initially meant to join us for Sahur, but plans changed, and he shared that night with us. Despite being two years younger, Yasser has been my closest friend through every season of life. We weren't always this way—our childhood was filled with fights, loud arguments, and sibling rivalry that sometimes felt endless. However, at some point, our disagreements became less intense, and our relationship grew stronger into an unbreakable friendship.

Yasser possesses a rare combination of acute intelligence and intense sensitivity. His heart's benevolence contrasts brilliantly with his analytical and logical attitude. I still recall coming across the question, *"What's the most painful thing you've ever experienced?"* one day, looking through his high school yearbook. I was halted when he said, *"I can see tears in my sister's eyes."* I recognized the essence of our relationship—a love so profound that it went beyond his austere exterior—in that straightforward, sincere response.

As an adult, Yasser became the CEO of a leading company, but even in leadership, his gentleness remains unchanged. Beneath the strength he projects lies a heart brimming with compassion. He is not just my brother; he's my rock—someone I know will always have my back, no matter how turbulent life becomes.

One of our adolescent memories is particularly clear. I discovered Yasser lying on his bed, sobbing over heartbreak, after he had called me into his room. I was reminded that my strong, calm brother had a fragile heart that felt deeply when I saw him so vulnerable. Our relationship became even closer during those intense emotional occasions.

Through all the highs and lows, Yasser has been a constant source of friendship and support. His presence has been a beacon of light that has helped me get through some of my darkest times and has reminded me that family is about more than just genetic ties, it's about consistently supporting one another.

· · · ● · ● · ● · ·

Talal was going to a fencing competition that evening, so Yasser had arranged to accompany him to Riyadh. Yasser asked Talal to accompany him by car even though he had a flight scheduled initially. Talal called his father and informed him of the change, saying, *"Yasser and I will be traveling by road; he is also going to Riyadh."* They might break their fast on the road, and they intended to depart about Iftar time. It was midday on Wednesday, October 27, and none of us had anticipated their presence for Sahur.

Yasser paid my mother a visit at her hospital workplace prior to their departure, probably to request money or other supplies for the trip. Yasser slipped away without saying goodbye as my mom went out to answer a business call. A sense of unease crept over her when she came back and saw he was gone. With a brief but significant concern that persisted in her heart, she thought, *"If something happens to him, I will never forgive myself."*

Yasser made a small stop by my father's house to pick up sandwiches made by my stepmother as a roadside supper to break their fast before heading to see Talal. Yasser left after bidding my father farewell for the last time. However, destiny stepped in. Yasser's car was violently hit by another motorist at a traffic light. The car was damaged sufficiently to interfere with their plans, even if he was unharmed.

Heartbroken, Yasser called Talal to give an explanation. He had to travel to the police station to finish the accident paperwork because he was no longer able to accompany him.

I experienced a surge of shock and dread when I initially learned about Yasser's accident. My rock, my brother, had been in an automobile accident! However, I was immediately relieved to learn that he was safe and that the automobile was the only thing damaged. Even so, he would come to Sahur with us that evening.

• • • ● • ● • • •

I stayed at my mom's house during that time, as my parents divorced. My friends arrived to pick me up, and we headed to Sahur at Aunt May's house. My mom had planned to join us, but she never showed up. I could only imagine how shaken she must have been after Yasser's accident, with her concern for him weighing heavily on her mind.

While I was at Sahur with my friends, my mother stayed home and spoke to a friend on the phone. She described the day's events, including how Yasser had come to say goodbye, how she had lost the opportunity to properly say goodbye to him, and how the possibility of something bad happening to him troubled her. *"Fortunately, Yasser is fine and enjoying Sahur with the family,"* her buddy told her. Her friend then inquired, almost as an afterthought, *"Have you called to check on Talal? Did he reach Riyadh safely?"* My mom replied, *"No, not yet. I should call him and make sure he's okay."*

Mom tried calling Talal several times, but his phone was off. Growing uneasy, she decided to call Aunt Dina. *"Have you heard from Talal?"* she asked. Aunt Dina's casual reply— *"No, not yet. I haven't—did* little to ease her worry. Mom sensed something was wrong then but couldn't have imagined how much worse it would become.

· · · ●· ● ●· ·

As I sat with my friends in Aunt May's garden, surrounded by laughter and gentle Arabic music, Aunt Dina descended the stairs in a beautiful *Jalabiya*, her blonde hair cascading to one side. *"Has anyone heard from Talal?"* she asked casually. While others dismissed the question, an unshakable feeling gripped me: *"He's not okay."* Yasser brushed it off, saying he hadn't heard from Talal yet. But the atmosphere had shifted for me. The lively chatter around me faded, replaced by an overwhelming sense of unease. My instincts screamed that something was wrong, and worry consumed me no matter how much I tried to stay present.

I crept upstairs to my cousin's dimly lit room in order to get away from the commotion. I repeatedly dialed Talal's number while gripping my phone hard in my shaking hand. My chest grew heavier with each unanswered ring, making it harder for me to breathe. I didn't know if Yasser, Mom, or Aunt Dina were calling him, too, but I did know that I had to hear Talal's voice. It seemed to be the only thing that could break through the oppressive fear that was growing inside of me. Time seemed to stand still in that room, with uncertainty weighing down every moment.

Like a weight dragging me down, a piercing agony twisted in my stomach, as though my belly was shouting something I couldn't quite make out. I attempted to steady my breathing while curled up against the wall with my legs pulled close, but nothing could stop the fear from eating at me. Two days ago, Talal called, but I didn't pick up. With a great weight of guilt bearing down on me, I kept thinking about that missed call. How come I didn't pick it up? The question kept coming back to me as I repeatedly rang his number, the pain growing with each ring that went unanswered. The soft hum of distant laughing and the serene glimmer of fairy lights outside seemed planets away. What should have been a joyful night had turned into a silent, hopeless hunt for hope in the darkness.

Even though I was terrified, I held on to a slender strand of hope while I sat by myself in that pitch-black chamber. I was afraid of losing Talal and having to face the truth, which I wasn't prepared for. An inexplicable ache weighed heavily on my chest, and the stillness surrounding me only heightened the fear that was building inside of me.

As we sat together, phones on speaker, dialing and redialing his number, my pals joined me, their presence a silent comfort. Every ring was a sliver of optimism that was swiftly extinguished by the crushing weight of yet another call that went unanswered. We held onto the hope that perhaps, just possibly, he was speaking to someone else while the line was busy. However, we felt in our hearts that the weight of the fact that so many people were attempting to contact him at once was intolerable.

The minutes stretched into eternity as the hours sluggishly passed. With each unanswered call, the walls pressed closer, making the space feel oppressive. I remained there in that oppressive silence from 10:30 PM to 1 AM until my friend Najla said she was going.

Aunt May's home, which had once been filled with love and joy, now seemed to be haunted by specters of doubt. I couldn't endure remaining indoors any longer. I noticed a sudden difference as soon as I stepped outdoors into the chilly night air: the joyous glow of the fairy lights outside contrasted with the oppressive weight on my chest. In its own way, the silence outside felt oppressive rather than consoling. I had to go. I could no longer remain encircled by the conflict between fear and happiness.

I followed Najla into the night and snuck out without saying farewell to anyone. I had a strong, unwavering sense that something wasn't right. However, I wasn't prepared to acknowledge it, not even to myself.

The only sound that broke the hush of the automobile ride was my repeated dialing of Talal's number. With each unanswered ring, my heart sank as my attention was fixed on my phone.

Then Najla's phone buzzed. She answered quietly, her voice barely above a whisper as she turned towards the window, her face hidden in the faint glow of passing streetlights. When she hung up, she said softly, *"Ahmad, I have to go."* Her tone was heavy, final—something about that call felt ominous. I didn't ask. I couldn't.

• • • ● • ● • • • •

Najla dropped me off at my mother's house and hugged me tightly, her voice low and heavy with sadness. *"Dalia, my brother passed by a serious accident on the road to Riyadh."*

My chest tightened. *"What car was it?"* I asked quickly.

"An Audi," she replied.

My voice trembled. *"Can he go back and check if it's Talal?"*

Najla shook her head softly. *"He's already in Riyadh, Dalia. That was hours ago."*

Reality struck like a thunderclap—this wasn't recent. Whatever had happened was already written in time.

I stood at my mother's doorstep, my hand resting on the doorknob. I paused there for a moment, trying to steady myself to prepare for whatever was waiting on the other side.

As the story progressed, tension was building at my mother's house. I was still upstairs in my cousin's dark room, clutching my phone and trying desperately to contact Talal. Family members dialed number after number downstairs, speaking softly and with the weight of unanswered questions on their faces.

My uncle didn't respond when my mother, shaking with anxiety, tried to contact him. Instead, in a frantic attempt to obtain information, she called my uncle's wife. *"Do you know anything about Talal?"* she asked, her voice breaking with concern.

The call with my uncle's wife became a moment captured in time as a silent storm grew on the other end of the line. I could hear her muffled sobs through the phone, sharp and raw. *"Oh my God, Yasmine, I don't know what to say. I don't know how to tell you,"* she finally choked out.

My mother's voice trembled as she asked, *"What's going on? Please tell me."*

Only a reply that shattered the delicate air between them could break the deafening quiet that followed: *"May he rest in peace."*

Clarity didn't arrive, but the words struck like a sudden, forceful wave. *"Who?"* my mother stumbled. *"Who are you referring to?"*

The reality weighed heavily on my uncle's wife, who hesitated on the other end. She was aware that what she was going to say would permanently shatter our world.

After a moment of hesitation, my uncle's wife asked my mother, *"Where is Yasser?"*

My mother said, perplexed, *"Yasser is here. Why? What's the matter?"*

"Yasser didn't go to Riyadh?" my uncle's wife said, her voice getting tighter with each word.

"No, he was unable to travel due to an accident that occurred this afternoon," my mother's voice was shaking now as she whispered, *"He's here."*

In bits and pieces, she realized that my uncle and his wife had been aware of the accident but had remained silent because they thought Yasser had been with Talal.

Desperate to find out, my mother asked the question she was scared to ask: *"Where's Talal?"*

The slow response cut like a knife through the silence. *"Your brother was summoned to the police station to be picked up."*

She gasped. *"Is he... is he dead?"*

The answer hung heavy in the air. *"I don't know."*

Desperate for answers, my mother called Aunt Dina. *"I've been trying to reach your brother. Could you please call him?"* Her voice trembled, heavy with uncertainty and fear.

"Talal's had accidents before; he'll be fine," Aunt Dina said nonchalantly, unaware of the seriousness of the situation. Unaware of the impact of my mother's silence, she carried on speaking in a pleasant tone. With dread creeping deeper into her chest, my mother gripped the phone and felt the world shrink around her.

As if to filter out the impact of what she was about to say, my mother stood motionless with one hand firmly placed against her brow. Her voice faltered as she tried to find a way to gently break the indescribable truth and help Aunt Dina transition from a momentary hope to irreparable loss.

However, Aunt Dina, who was still oblivious, continued to talk softly, her words barely grazing the brink of a terrible truth.

The brittle silence was finally broken by my mother's voice. *"Enough, Dina. I hope he finds peace."*

The final, uncompromising words weighed thick in the air.

• • • ● • ● • • •

Across the room, my younger brother Faisal froze, his face buried in his hands, his shoulders trembling under the weight of understanding. My mother let the phone slip from her fingers as though it had become too heavy to hold.

Through the faint crackle of the call, Aunt Dina's scream shattered the silence, raw and piercing. I stood there, paralyzed, as the sound echoed into every corner of the house. The room was swallowed by silence—a silence so heavy it felt alive, pressing down on all of us.

"Why did I not cherish those last chances to say goodbye properly?" Persistent in prayer, I hoped—*"please, let this all be a mistake, a misunderstanding."*

The weight of the reality split something inside of me and started me to cry uncontrollably. I staggered into my room, dropped to my knees, and stared up at the ceiling as though it contained solutions. *"Please, God,"* I said silently, *"let this be a mistake. Allow this to be a nightmare."* But the silence that followed felt definitive, and no prayer could undo the already set action.

I was grieving, fierce, and relentless. As if physical suffering might somehow wash out the sorrow thundering in my chest, I smacked my face and banged my fists against my legs.

Somewhere in the haze, my mother's shaky voice cut through the silence, *"Dina, enough. Azamallah Ajrik. I hope his soul finds peace."*

I turned to face Faisal, who had tears running down his cheeks and his face crumpled with wordless sadness. Something sharp and illogical ignited within me. *"What's causing your tears?"* I yelled, my voice shaking with desperation and rage. *"She is insane; don't listen to her!"*

But denial cracked and splintered inside me even as I said it, and the floodgates opened wide. My mind spun in wild, desperate circles. *"Please, God, I'll do anything—pray more, wear the hijab, anything—just don't let this be real."*

The sound of an automobile engine approaching broke through the brittle quiet. Hurrying to the window, I froze. Rising from the automobile were Yasser and Fareed. My breath seized in my throat, and I swiftly covered my mouth with a hand to stifle the cries that threatened to flee. Not yet, not like this—I couldn't let Yasser hear me crying.

I cleaned my face, inhaled, quivering, then walked outside to see him. Time seemed to stop the instant our eyes crossed. As Yasser begged, his face collapsed, and his voice cracked: *"Dalia... no, no, no... Please don't tell me..."*

I ran mute. My quiet was louder than any word I could have used. Desperate and chiseled into every motion, he shook his head fiercely, his hand brushing past me as he shoved his way into the home. Fareed staggered behind him, his face white and his steps erratic. With our shared silence bearing the intolerable weight of what we already knew, I grasped his arm and guided him inside.

· · · · ● · ● · · · ·

The following five hours vanished into a blur—a hollow stretch where everything felt too fast and painfully slow.

When awareness returned, I found myself in the car, the early morning light creeping over the horizon as we headed towards Riyadh.

Couldn't Say Goodbye
The Pain of Unspoken Words and Missed Farewells

After that evening, everything faded into a hazy blur. I can't recall when Yasser came to terms with the awful reality, no matter how hard I tried to piece it together. Mom doesn't recall either, despite my asking. Our minds seem to have worked together to shield us from such intolerable situations.

I know we were together—Mom, Yasser, and I—locked in a shared reality too devastating to face head-on. Those moments must have been some of the worst we've ever endured, but my memory has mercifully erased them.

Eventually, the phone began to ring. Calls came in about traveling to Riyadh to be with my grandfather for the funeral.

I felt hollow, numb—like a zombie walking through a world stripped of color.

"Dalia, go pack your things," Mom's sharp and distant voice broke through the fog.

I walked in a robotic manner, mindlessly packing clothes into a suitcase. No matter what I grabbed, it was either black shirts or black jeans. My head was stuck in an unbreakable haze, and my body went through the motions.

In those moments, I felt as though Talal had been buried with a piece of my childhood. A light had gone out, and the world would never be the same.

But still, I kept moving—one foot in front of the other—because stopping wasn't an option.

Packing for Riyadh felt like a dream—or, more accurately, a nightmare. My mind was detached, floating far away as my hands stuffed black shirts and pants into a bag. They were all I owned anyway, and what I brought didn't matter.

Every movement felt mechanical, every breath heavy. I wasn't truly present—I was existing, going through the motions because stopping wasn't an option.

The next thing I remember, I was sitting beside her husband, Uncle Mahmoud, in the backseat of Aunt Dina's car. We were driving down the same cursed highway where Talal had taken his final breath.

I curled up in the corner of the seat, pressing my throbbing head against the cold glass of the window. The early morning sky was still dark as we pulled away—maybe 4 or 5 A.M.

Somewhere along that long, unending drive, I had an odd sense. I sensed Talal. Outside the window, his presence hung in the silent air. Desperately, I studied the deserted highway for any indication—his car, his silhouette—that would dispel this harsh reality.

Later, I learned that we had passed the exact location of the accident.

A terrible headache began to pulse behind my eyes, each throb a cruel echo of the pain tearing me apart inside. That headache would follow me relentlessly for five days, like a shadow I couldn't shake.

When we finally arrived at my grandfather's house in Riyadh—a house filled with my happiest childhood memories—it no longer felt warm or safe.

Every corner, every familiar smell, every creak in the floorboards carried Talal's ghost. His laughter echoed faintly in the spaces where we used to play.

However, I was unable to enter his bedroom. The hush that would greet me there was too much for me to handle. The wound in my chest felt like it would never heal, and the pain was still too intense.

A constant flow of sympathy visits flooded our home in the days following the funeral. The main area below was alive with whispered prayers, sobbing hugs, and quiet voices. However, I couldn't stand to see them.

Dim light filtered through the curtains of one of the bedrooms upstairs, where I took refuge. The quiet enveloped me like a thick shroud. The only way to get away from the unrelenting storm inside of me was to lie on the bed in that quiet, remote place.

I eventually had to look for medicine and drink since my head was throbbing so hard. I almost ran into my cousin Mohammed as I staggered into the corridor, dazed and hollow.

When he saw my swollen cheeks, the blotchy redness around my eyes, and the hollow expression in my gaze, his eyes softened.

He said, "*Dalia, please... not like this,*" his voice soft and his gaze cautious, as if I would break into a thousand pieces if he said something incorrectly.

I looked away, embarrassed by the mess I had become, even though every tear was etched into my face for all to see.

Despite shutting myself away, despite the hours spent curled in silence, acceptance still felt so far out of reach.

My soul became a broken record of bargaining, spinning in endless cycles with every whispered prayer.

"Please, God," I pleaded into the silence, *"I'll do anything—pray more, wear the hijab, give to charity every day—just please, please make this not real. I can't survive without him."*

I begged God in every way I could think of, whispering fervent prayers into the stillness. However, the globe would not budge in response to my entreaties, and the silence persisted. The realization that he was no longer with me crept slowly and cruelly into every nook and cranny of my thoughts.

I had to find a way to exist in a world without him, without the bright light that had guided me for so long.

Even as funeral preparations moved around me like shadows, my mind clung stubbornly to fleeting possibilities: *"What if he was lost somewhere in the desert? What if this was all a mistake?"*

I hadn't seen his body with my own eyes. That shred of denial became my fragile lifeline.

The morning after we arrived in Riyadh, the rest of the family went to the mosque to say their final goodbyes.

I stayed behind, frozen in place, paralyzed by the thought of seeing him lifeless. Whispers reached me later—about his broken nose, about how he might not look the same.

One part of me insisted I couldn't let that be my last image of him. But another voice screamed that I was a coward for not saying goodbye one last time.

Anger bubbled up when I realized no one had told me they were leaving for the mosque.

"Did they think I was too fragile? Too broken? Shouldn't I have had the choice?"

Even still, a second thought began to creep in: perhaps it was for the best.

There is no guide to grieving, no ideal method for surviving in this strange world. One breath at a time, survival was the sole option—there was no right or wrong decision.

· · · **·** · **·** · · ·

The house was deserted when I woke up.

"Where is everybody?" With a little hesitation in my voice, I questioned the nanny.

"They went to see Talal," she said quietly, averting her gaze from mine.

I was left in a bewildering whirlpool of emotions when the words struck me like a wave. I was happy that I didn't have to say goodbye for the last time. However, another part of me ached, as if I had been left out of something holy, my final opportunity to say goodbye.

The silence seemed cold and wide as I strolled downstairs and collapsed onto the couch in the living room.

My mind was racing with incessant queries. "*What are they up to now? Are they above him? Are they muttering prayers? Is Yasser surviving?*"

Yasser. My chest constricted at the mere thought of him. I imagined him marching solemnly with the others, possibly assisting in carrying Talal's body. I got a chill from the picture.

Since they were little, Talal and Yasser had been inseparable. I was certain that Yasser would bear the consequences of this catastrophe in a different way, allowing it to etch remorse into his very being.

His sanity was being eroded by those what-ifs, which I could practically hear eating away at him every second: "*I wish I had been in the vehicle that evening. I wish I hadn't recommended traveling by car. Would Talal remain present?*"

However, Yasser was calm and stoic, his sorrow confined behind a wall of silence.

The only holes in his armor were the quick looks he gave my grandfather, as though the loss of Talal was a scar on his soul, causing him to avoid his eyes.

I didn't realize the full scope of his suffering until years later.

Yasser had poured his heart out on the screen in a string of private emails to my parents and uncles, page after page of self-blame, sorrow, and guilt.

Yasser's emails revealed a deep well of guilt and self-blame, each sentence heavy with unspoken sorrow. His grief was a quiet storm, turning inward where mine had erupted outward.

While my grief had erupted outward—through rebellion, anger, and restless energy—Yasser's had turned inward, hardening into an impenetrable wall of silence and self-condemnation.

In those early days, I could see the light in Yasser's eyes dim, replaced by a quiet torment he refused to share with anyone. I realized strength wasn't always about resilience—it was sometimes just a brittle mask holding back an ocean of anguish.

When I pictured Yasser walking beside Talal's lifeless form during those final moments, a deep, overwhelming sadness washed over me.

Grief had left behind more than just broken hearts—it had scattered shards of guilt and regret, sharp enough to wound us long after the funeral was over.

I sensed, even then, that Yasser's burden was heavier than mine—a weight he carried in silence, without complaint, without release.

Years passed, and yet we never spoke of Talal. Our silence became a shared language, an unspoken agreement not to touch that still-bleeding wound.

It wasn't until recently that I felt ready to discuss that terrible time with him. But when I finally brought it up, Yasser's face remained a closed door—emotionless, distant, reserved.

Had he moved on? Had the grief faded for him while I remained frozen in time, anchored to the past?

Yasser claimed he remembered very little of those days. He described them vaguely, like faded scenes from a distant nightmare—a car accident, Aunt Dina's mourning feast.

His fragmented memories contrasted with my sharp recollections, and each detail was etched into me like a scar.

For a brief moment, I wondered, "Was *I the one clinging too tightly? Had I become trapped in grief while he had found a way to let go?*

However, it dawned on me that Yasser had remembered. He had decided to live. He had buried his memories deep, locked them tightly, and put them away so they could no longer harm him.

We had each carried our grief differently. Mine was loud and restless; his grief was quiet and unyielding.

But in the end, grief had made prisoners of us both—just in different cells.

• • • • • • • • • • •

While Yasser and some members of the family accompanied Talal's body on its final procession, I stayed behind at home with Mom.

The silence at home felt heavy, pressing against the walls and echoing in every corner. It was a stark contrast to the collective mourning at the burial site. I couldn't shake the feeling of absence, as if the air had been drained from the house.

Everyone else had left for the funeral ceremonies, so we woke up to silence. There was silence for hours, but then there were hints of word that Talal had been buried, and the prayers had ended.

The hours went by, with every second seeming to drag on forever. It felt like the definitive, irrevocable conclusion of a chapter as we heard the faint murmurs of the funeral rites. Now that Talal was gone, there was complete silence.

The gravity of loss had robbed the house of its normal warmth, leaving it achingly quiet.

"Who wants to lead the prayer for Talal's soul?" someone asked softly. The question hung heavy in the air and was met with silence.

Before I could fully comprehend what was happening, Mom gestured towards me.

My throat tightened, and my heart pounded painfully in my chest.

Though my faith had splintered into shards of bitterness and confusion, I was stepping into the moment. I guided the prayer from somewhere deep within—a hollow, numb space.

When it was over, I retreated upstairs, back into the sanctuary of my solitude.

I didn't want to see or talk to anyone. The faint murmur of broken prayers murmured into the darkness was the only sound in my room.

Despite the fact that I was surrounded by people, I felt completely alone. School friends came up to me and whispered condolences, but their features were fuzzy, and their words seemed far.

I gazed forward, empty and inaccessible, encased in the cocoon of my sorrow.

Maybe it was in those early days of silence that my grief solidified, turning into something immovable—something I carried with me for years.

Yasser and I grieved differently. He built a fortress around his sorrow, a wall so high that no one could reach him.

However, I was afraid to let go of my pain because I thought it was my last link to Talal, so I held it close to me like a delicate memento.

Thus, our sorrow turned into two distinct islands: remote and inaccessible, growing farther apart each year.

The weight of our loss broke something deep inside of us, leaving us stuck in our individual versions of purgatory, even though we had once shared an unbreakable tie.

· · · · ·· · ·· · ·

Those who did go said Talal appeared calm, even serene, in spite of his wounds. They claimed that he appeared to be just dozing off, with the tiniest hint of a smile on his lips.

They ought to have reassured me. They ought to have offered a resolution, a glimmer of calm among the mayhem. However, they didn't.

Rather, they stimulated my mind, which relentlessly crafted other scenarios and stories where Talal was still alive, and this wasn't real.

"Perhaps he had been abducted," I thought frantically. *"Perhaps he was waiting for us to find him out there, still breathing and alive."*

I refused to confront the truth, which was getting closer by the hour, and clung to these illusions like a lifeline.

I remained upstairs, confined in my self-imposed exile, as my family gathered for Talal's funeral, saying their final goodbyes and sharing a final kiss on his forehead.

He had the inevitability of death carved into his features, but I wasn't there to see him. And because I wasn't there, my mind was free to resist—free to create alternate endings to a story already written.

"If I didn't see it, maybe it didn't happen." That unbearable separation became my shield against reality, allowing me to preserve a fragile, flickering hope.

I could still think that Talal may enter the room again, his voice filling the gap, his grin beaming, as long as I could avoid that last, heartbreaking moment.

But I knew the truth in my heart. It was palpable to me, like a chilly burden in the pit of my stomach.

And so, I turned my desperation toward prayer—not with devotion, but with pleading, with bargaining.

"Please, God. Let this all be some kind of mistake. Please, let there be another ending to this story."

But no answer came. Only silence. And in that silence, the weight of reality grew heavier still.

"Please, let this all be a terrible mistake. Maybe Talal was lost or hurt somewhere, and we'd somehow get him back.

The prayers tumbled in a desperate stream, each word clinging to a threadbare hope.

I opened my email at some point. I don't know what compelled me, but an old Talal message from about a week before had prompted me.

For a split second, my heart leaped. *"He's alive! He just emailed me!"*

But then I noticed the date stamp. The harsh, unalterable date.

It was a relic, not a lifeline. A fossil from before the world fell apart.

I sat shaking in the present, attempting to cling to something that had already passed, while his words stared back at me, frozen in time.

Absorbing the finality of his death was like walking through thick fog—slow, disorienting, and suffocating.

Three days later, reality delivered its final, crushing blow.

Dad called. His voice broke in ways I had never heard before.

For the first time in my life, I heard Dad sobbing in public. Talal had maintained a special place in his heart despite their divorce—a connection unbreakable by time or distance.

My uncle later told me about the incident in a tearful voice: *"Your father...he couldn't stop crying at the funeral."* It was really challenging for him.

I was held together by those words, which sliced through the final thread. Like sand, the denial that had kept me afloat slid from my fingertips.

Talal was gone. Really, truly gone.

No prayer, no bargain, no whispered plea could change it.

The bargaining that consumed my every waking moment—the desperate prayers, wild theories, and hopeful illusions—collapsed into anger: "*Why him? Why now? Why our family?*"

I raged at the universe, fate, and every invisible force I could imagine.

At just 21 years old, I was forced to confront the cracks in my faith. I still believed in a higher power, but that belief had been scorched, twisted, and made fragile by grief.

In those moments, I realized that faith is not a shield against pain. Sometimes, it's just the smallest flicker of light in the darkest corner of an unbearable night.

I searched for solace in faith, feeling untethered and adrift. I longed for comfort and answers but found only silence where I expected reassurance. The silence that let the judgmental prayers and empty platitudes be brushed aside.

In those early years of adulthood, I hunted desperately for spiritual meaning, trying to patch the cavernous void Talal's death had left behind.

But when the grief became too heavy, when the silence became too loud, my soul defaulted to anger and isolation.

In the quietest hours of the night, I found myself whispering questions into the dark: "*Why did this happen? Why him? Why now? Did he suffer? Was there any meaning to this pain?*"

The questions echoed inside me, unanswered, until they became an exhausting loop of torment.

When no answers came—when all that remained was silence—cynicism crept in, filling every hollowed-out corner of my spirit.

While I lay tossing in restless sleep, a loud slam jolted me awake one night. My heart thundered in my chest as I bolted upright and rushed to the door, flinging it open. The hallway was empty, still, and eerily silent. Then, from somewhere distant, the call to prayer began to echo through the quiet house.

For a fleeting moment, I felt something—a connection, an invisible thread pulling me toward the rituals Talal had cherished. But sorrow is heavy, and my spirit was too burdened with rising. Defiantly, I turned away from the quiet invitation and crawled back into bed, pulling the blankets around me like armor.

If Talal's presence lingered in those moments, I refused to acknowledge it.

I was too angry, too broken to let faith back into the fragile ruins of my heart.

During those empty days of bereavement, I stayed imprisoned in my chamber.

Friends and relatives arrived and left, their footfalls gentle and their voices hushed. Still, I stayed far, isolating myself even more and keeping anyone from closing the distance from my grief.

• • • ● ● ● ● ● • •

Grandfather and Aunt Dina were the only individuals I paid attention to; they were both ensnared in their terrifying plunges into the merciless depths of despair.

His once lively energy had now faded into a hollow shell, and Grandfather was still slouched on the couch in the living room, highly medicated. His quiet pain was so loud that it reverberated throughout the entire house.

Aunt Dina, however, allowed her pain to fill every available space. One afternoon, as she called Aunt Maysa from hundreds of miles away, her cries rang out through the walls and shattered my seclusion.

As she attempted to comfort her younger sister across the eerie gap of distance and grief, I could practically see her face contorted in pain, her eyes red and swollen, and her voice breaking.

Grief was a raging storm in those early years. Even the simplest tasks, including breathing, eating, and simply existing, felt impossible.

I don't remember who convinced me to come downstairs on the last day of mourning. But somehow, I found myself walking into the main gathering area, numb and disoriented.

To console our shattered, family, friends, and neighbors had traditionally offered food platters. The delicious aroma of spiced lamb filled the air. I grabbed a plate, proceeded automatically, and then took a bite.

I froze the instant the flesh hit my tongue. I had the impression that I was devouring Talal—his very being, his energy, his essence.

Acidic and stinging, panic swept through me. I dropped the plate, staggered to the bathroom, and threw up so hard that my throat was raw and my stomach was empty.

However, the odor persisted—the unyielding ghost of that one bite tormenting my senses.

I couldn't look at meat for months after that without feeling disgusted. Sharp and unforgiving, the recollection of that instant lingered in my body.

But in between the dry heaves and the shudders, an odd clarity crept in.

It seemed as if I had cleansed something more than the physical, as if I had thrown out the dregs of a past existence in which Talal was still alive.

The smallest glimmer of resolve stirred in my chest as I stumbled out of the bathroom, exhausted.

It felt monumental to take that tentative step back toward the crowd of mourners downstairs.

I knew that I would always be grieving. Every moment would be tinged with the shadows of anger, despair, and denial.

But I started to slither forward with just one stride.

I began the laborious process of piecing together the pieces of my broken reality to create something that would be able to bear Talal's absence.

• • • ● • ● • ● • • •

Mom, Sara, Yusra, Dina, May, and other of my cousins rounded Grandpa's house's kitchen bar. Though it had been a few days since the funeral, the weight of loss loomed large and oppressive.

Uncle Sarry arrived, his face worn with tiredness, the creases on his forehead deepening under the weight he carried. He stopped, inhaling deeply as though he were preparing himself for what he was going to say.

"There is a saying from the Prophet," he said, his voice both firm and brittle, *"When a man dies, his good deeds are finished, except for three things: a running charity, knowledge that benefits others after him, or a righteous child who prays for him."*

The room went completely quiet, his comments soaking into every one of us like stones. *"Talal didn't have children of his own, but he has righteous siblings, nieces, and nephews who will continue praying for his soul,"* Uncle Sarry said with a little faltering voice.

His calm façade crumbled for a split second, and I saw the unvarnished loss he had been suppressing. But he straightened, gathered himself, and attempted to be the pillar of strength we all required—quiet dignity.

Later, I would learn the weight of everything he had carried in those days. Uncle Sarry had been the one to receive the call—the devastating call summoning him to the police station to identify Talal's body. I couldn't fathom what it must have felt like to drive those two long hours, dread gnawing at him with every mile that passed.

But it didn't end there. Uncle Sarry also carried the intolerable responsibility of delivering the news to Grandpa. He struggled to pronounce those terrible words aloud. Knowing the news could break Grandpa's delicate heart, he contacted Dr. Mazin, his cardiologist. Arriving carrying a sedative, the doctor gently delivered the truth.

Uncle Sarry turned into the calm anchor, keeping the family together while we were lost in the fog of our grief. Despite his own sad heart, he made sure Grandpa was taken care of, managed logistics for the mourners who gathered in great numbers, and planned burial plans.

Still, Uncle Sarry was not immune to the frays of loss. I noticed flashes of it carved on his face, little cracks in an otherwise austere mask. Still, he never let those fissures get wider. He carried all—his loss, ours, and the weight of keeping our family afloat over a storm none of us had been ready for.

Grandpa waited anxiously in the living room for Talal to come through the door, as he did every night. Although the hours passed, he asked no questions. He waited, his heart silently clutching hope, his gaze riveted on the door.

Grandpa raised his head, expecting, until finally, a knock broke the stillness. His cardiologist, Dr. Mazin, showed up instead of Talal. "What do you wish?" Grandpa growled, his voice sharp with mistrust.

Dr. Mazin paused momentarily before moving gently ahead. He knew, as a cardiologist, that the terrible news he conveyed might be fatal for Grandpa's weak heart. He gave Grandpa a small sedative before speaking, his words quiet and methodical as he softly said Talal was gone.

That image—Grandpa's hopeful waiting turning into devastating loss—tightened my stomach into knots.

During those times, I came to understand the tremendous strength required to withstand the intolerable while everyone else around fell apart. Knowing he would have to calm Grandpa's collapsing world, I couldn't understand how Uncle Sarry managed to organize the precise orchestration of that moment—getting the doctor there first, getting ready for the aftermath.

Uncle Sarry started to be the family's reluctant messenger right then. For the mourners who showed up in great numbers to pay their respects, he planned the funeral activities, organized burial preparations, and supervised logistics—food, beverages, and lodging. He simultaneously took great care of Grandpa, whose loss had made him a delicate shadow of himself.

Uncle added, his voice firm but tense, "*Talal had righteous siblings, nieces, and nephews who would carry that duty; he had no children to pray for him.*"

That little break in his austere façade exposed the terrible weight of his responsibility. Being the sole surviving son, he had to keep the family together while carrying his sadness like a leaden shroud.

I remember looking at Uncle that day at the kitchen bar. His face was carved with exhaustion, and his shoulders seemed permanently hunched under the invisible weight he carried. It was as though he had aged years in just a matter of days. His customary friendliness and charm had faded, replaced by a calm, steely determination.

Uncle Sarry lacked the luxury of withdrawing into a lonely cocoon of rage and incredulity as I did. Duty had eaten his grief, guiding us constantly through a tempest that might have pulled us all under.

For a split second, I watched the flutter of suffering over his face—the smallest breach in his well-kept façade. Then he straightened, inhaled steadily, and kept us moving ahead.

I realized then the resiliency that had kept our family intact through every difficulty. No matter how insurmountable it seemed, we would survive this calamity. Uncle Sarry would ensure that. For him, failing was not an alternative.

· · · ● · ● · · ·

Days after the funeral, I started to feel an unusual emptiness. The feverish turmoil of those first few days of grief gave way to a murky despair, weighty and aimless. Where in this shadow-ridden world is Talal's light to lead us?

Hidden in solitary isolation upstairs, one afternoon, muted whispers from a group of mourners floated up to where I sat. Their low voices transmitted bits of stories, recollections of Talal, and hushed words of comfort never quite reaching me. Only listening, though, silent, calm, and hollowed out by loss.

Some women mumbled back and forth about remembering *"what a special kid"* Talal had been. Their statements, veiled in subdued tones of sympathy and condolence, set off a fierce anger inside me.

These outsiders were meant to bring Talal's vivid life down to a series of dead platitudes? How can they reduce his genius, his luminosity, into just another hollow narrative of tragic young death—just another transitory story to be handed around in sad whispers?

Their cleaned-up language failed to convey the weight of his presence, the depth of his affection, or how his energy lit every place he entered. From someplace deep inside me, white-hot rage burst through the shell I had worked so hard to keep intact.

Every rebel impulse shouted at me to march downstairs, to face them, to set their empty condolences ablaze with the primal fire of my loss. But something kept me back—an unseen thread of restriction. I stayed frozen in place, jaws gritted, fists balled, and every angry syllable swallowed down into the pit of my stomach instead of spiraling into a maelstrom of wrath.

From that point on, my voice became a delicate liability—a wild, uncontrollable energy that had to be imprisoned and muffled. I did not trust myself to speak without my sadness erupting in a tidal wave of fury and destruction. I so did the one thing I could: mute myself.

I turned off every impulse to communicate the whirl of need, grief, and wrath twisted inside me. I went within, stone by stone, building an impenetrable wall around my emotions until I had become untouchable. By doing this, I became a ghost—a shell of the person I had been. My soul was too delicate to risk exposure, so I wandered the planet in a calm fog, observing life pass by but being emotionally absent. Every time I dared to let my guard down, silence became my haven, my refuge against the unrelenting riptide of loss threatening to draw me under.

· · · ● · ● · · ·

A few days later, we were all gathered at Grandpa's house. Mom, my aunts, and I sat together upstairs in the green room. This room had been Talal's childhood sanctuary, where we cousins had spent endless hours wrapped in laughter and imaginary adventures. Even now silent, the walls seemed to throb with the echoes of those happy days.

My head lost in a cloud of grief, I sat by the window staring blankly at the world outside. The subdued voices from downstairs and the slight creak of the floorboards were hardly noticed.

Mom's soft voice sliced through the fog. *"Dalia, it will get better,"* she replied gently, squeezing my hand. *"God says, 'There is ease with every difficulty."* Good things are on their way.

Her comments were a flutter of light in the dungeon of my loss, a warmth I hadn't felt in days.

"Like what?" My voice was shaky and small, I asked.

She started to smile faintly, her eyes glittering with brittle hope.

She continued, her voice gentle and almost prophetic, *"Maybe you'll get married soon."*

Her comments at the time seemed to be a far-off fantasy, a flimsy thread of hope against the weight of loss.

I had no idea how prophetic those statements would turn out.

• • • ● • ● • ● • • •

Days after Talal's death, we gathered for another funeral in Aunt May's exquisite Khobar house. Once radiating warmth and celebration, the elaborate decorations felt hollow and lost, like echoes of a joy gone from us.

Aunt May glided elegantly among groups of guests, providing comfort and hospitality even as she grieved her brother. Though flimsy and pasted, her smile never wavered. How she called that strength still baffles me.

I sat curled in my corner and watched the familiar faces all around. These were the same friends who had gently surrounded me with encouragement just a few days ago. Now, though, their presence seemed far-off, as if they had turned into subdued onlookers to a sadness they were unable to access.

On the memorial prayer booklet, my fingers blindly followed Talal's face's outline. His picture turned back at me, peaceful and unspoiled by the terrible destiny fate had chosen. I couldn't get myself to read the words posted next to his photo. Rather, I hung his picture, learning every curve and nuance as though it may somehow bring him back to me.

A small figure emerged from the corner of my eye into my peripheral vision. In his early years, Talal had cared deeply for a girl whose presence brought out his warmest smiles and brightest moments.

Her delicate face twisted as she battled tears, her serenity wavering under the weight of her anguish. I yearned for her to let go—to crumble, cry honestly, and break in a way I hadn't let myself do.

Didn't she deserve to scream, mourn, and express the full weight of the injustice we had all been forced to bear?

Her arms almost grazed my shoulders in a subdued hug as she at last traversed the room and stopped before me. Still, oceans of loss swept between us even in that modest act.

For a while, I questioned whether seeing her break down would help me to validate my loss—if seeing someone else shoulder the intolerable weight would make my load somewhat less heavy. Or maybe, I realized, she mourned so delicately because she feared being left alone with the remnants of a bond no one else could truly understand.

The prayer booklet felt unbearably heavy in my hands, its weight pressing down on me like the crushing finality of Talal's absence.

With tear-filled eyes, I stared at her, and for a brief minute, we shared the quiet of two souls permanently altered by loss.

Was giving her the proper moral direction? She was simply a small girl, rather young. But I felt she ought to see his face one final time.

I inhaled deeply and turned over the brochure to her.

"*Look at him,*" I whispered gently, shaking with compassion and urgency.

She initially moved slowly. Her small hands held the booklet's edges, and her eyes were fixed on the cover, but she did not glance beyond it.

"*Please look,*" I said, my voice harsher this time, snapping with frustration—not at her, but at the terrible reality we were both being forced to face.

At last, she opened the brochure with shaking hands. Her eyes fixed on Talal's face, locked eternally in the pictures—a face so familiar, so adored.

She let out a hard, biting sob that broke through the stillness of the room. That held the weight of innocence broken and tragic in real time and is a sound I will never forget.

Tears flowed down her bright cheeks and landed on the glossy pages as she gripped the booklet to her bosom as though she were clutching Talal personally.

I pulled her nearby, reaching forward and encircling her little, delicate figure. Her cries muffled against me as my tears followed quiet pathways down my cheeks. She buried her face into my shoulder.

For what felt like an eternity—two souls joined together in grief—anchored by loss and love—we stayed like that.

The rest of the funeral became a haze; a never-ending stream of people, words, and rites passed by without leaving a mark.

I went across it all like a shadow, numb and hollow, hardly connected to the surroundings.

My grief was so weighty it felt like a second skin, as if I were a ghost moving among a sea of bereaved people.

· · · ● · ● · · ·

One year later, I was married and beginning an interesting new phase. But that day I nodded, caught in the whirl of grief.

On what should have been one of the happiest days of my life, I carried a weight in my chest that no celebration could lift. I smiled in photographs, exchanged words with guests, and fulfilled every bride's expectation—but there was a shadow behind every laugh. Talal's absence clung to me, invisible but ever-present.

Returning to college after the funeral was no easier. In my psychology class, the topic of grief came up one day, and it was as if someone had torn the fragile stitches holding me together.

The lecturer talked in a clinical, steady voice, yet every syllable sliced like glass into me. I left, not able to stay. I pushed my chair back, the screaming sound tearing through the still classroom. Eyes pointed at me, laden with inquiry and worry.

As I hurried outside, the hallways speeding by me burned on my face. I felt naked and vulnerable; my loss was on show for everyone.

Slumping on an old corridor couch, I tried to get some air outside. Still, the sobbing arrived—uninvited and relentless.

One of my classmates trailed behind me—a girl whose face bore her interpretation of sadness. She sat next to me silently, and we both started to cry. Something went between us in that wordless conversation—a brittle link created by common suffering. I came to see that loss speaks to everyone.

But even as I moved forward—through marriage, classes, ticking minutes, and years—one thing haunted me: regret. I kept replaying those last moments with Talal over and over in my mind. *"Why didn't I answer his call that day?"* It was a question that pulsed in the back of my mind like a relentless drumbeat.

I could still see his name lighting up on my phone screen. I could still feel the cool breeze coming through my window and hear the faint hum of distant traffic. *"I'll call him back later,"* I had told myself. But *"later"* never came.

Those final missed moments became an unhealed wound, a constant ache I carried everywhere.

Talal had been a lifeline during one of the darkest times of my life. My parents' divorce had shattered my sense of stability, leaving me raw and uncertain.

He called me every day, checking in, his voice warm and steady. He had been my anchor, my safe space. *"How are you doing?"* he would ask.

But I had been too drained, too caught in my pain to answer him that final time.

I carried that regret with me through every milestone, every triumph, every moment of joy.

Time has softened the sharp edges of my grief, but it has not erased it. Grief, I've learned, isn't something you overcome—it's something you carry.

It becomes a part of you, stitched into the fabric of who you are.

Talal's absence is a shadow that walks beside me, a whisper in quiet moments, a presence I feel in the spaces he once filled.

But it's also love—enduring, unbroken, and eternal.

"I'll carry you with me, Talal. Always."

And in that quiet promise, I found a fragile peace—a way to honor and keep him close, even as I continued moving forward in a world he no longer inhabited.

A Brother By Choice
The Bond That Went Beyond Blood

Talal's upbringing was enriched by a diverse heritage spanning Saudi Arabia, Palestine, Germany, and France. This multicultural background played a significant role in shaping his unique identity. Talal's deep care and closeness to his family were always evident, from funny childhood moments to heartfelt conversations.

My grandfather was an extraordinary doctor who studied medicine in Germany for 14 years. While there, he met and married my grandmother, and they had my mother. However, their marriage didn't last. After their separation, my grandfather remarried—twice—to two incredible German women who became beloved grandmothers and mother figures in our family. When Grandpa eventually returned to Riyadh with his two wives, he brought my mother with him, separating her from her birth mother. I can only imagine how scared and heartbroken my mom must have felt as a little girl, leaving her mother behind. But my second grandmother stepped in with love and strength, raising my mother with care and resilience.

Despite the complexities of their family dynamic, my mother grew up alongside her step-siblings—Sarry and Dina—and later Brigette, who gave her four stepsisters: May, Maysa, Yusra, and Sara. They were united by deep love, loyalty, and unwavering support for one another, a bond that would later extend to Talal when he became part of our lives.

• • • ● • ● • • •

Sara and I were born in the same year, 1983. Technically, she's my aunt, but we grew up more like sisters. Just three months older than me, Sara was my closest friend from the very start. We spent countless hours at my grandfather's big house, where our days were filled with laughter, play, and endless adventures.

Sara felt like the sister I never had—a partner in mischief, a confidante, and my first best friend. Together, we created a world of shared secrets and cherished memories, building an inseparable bond that still warms my heart today.

When I was about seven years old, someone new came into our lives—Talal. Grandpa had married again, this time to a half-German, half-French lady. His first three wives were all German, but his fourth wife was different. Talal's mom lived in France, and Talal was a secret known only to my mother; none of her siblings knew about his existence.

When my mom first met Talal, she felt an odd mix of curiosity and responsibility. Already raising her son Yasser, who was just a few months older than Talal, she instinctively stepped into a nurturing role. At first, Talal didn't seem like her brother—more like another child she needed to care for. But soon enough, their bond deepened, and Talal became a beloved part of our family dynamic.

When Talal turned five, Grandpa brought him from France to live with us in Riyadh. That was when the rest of my aunts and uncles met their baby brother for the first time. My mother formed a quick and deep bond with Talal. Having been separated from her mother as a child, she deeply understood his unspoken feelings of loss and confusion.

Grandpa's decision to bring Talal and my mother under one roof wasn't arbitrary. He wanted to raise all his children together, hoping they would grow up united, with strong sibling bonds despite the complexities of their family dynamic.

Looking back, I'm grateful for the day Talal joined our family. His presence added a new layer of warmth, love, and laughter to our lives. I'm glad our family had a new little "brother" that day.

· · · ● · ● · · ·

One of my earliest memories is the first time I met Talal. I was around seven years old, and he was five. I remember walking into Grandpa's big house and spotting a tiny boy across the room. His pale, freckled skin and bright red hair stood out against the familiar tones of our family's features. He looked so small and fragile, like a delicate porcelain doll come to life.

"*Who's this new kid?*" I must have wondered. At that age, I had no idea he was family. He was just an adorable, milk-white stranger suddenly appearing in our world. Looking back, I can't imagine how bewildering it must have been for Talal, too. After spending his early years in Europe, he was now surrounded by a bustling Arabic family in a foreign environment.

But any awkwardness faded quickly. Yasser and I welcomed Talal into our lives with open arms. Being the two youngest boys, Yasser and Talal bonded instantly, becoming inseparable partners in crime. Meanwhile, Sara and I, the two eldest girls, were an inseparable duo.

The four of us—Sara, Yasser, Talal, and I—became a team. Whether we dressed in ridiculous costumes, played endless games of hide-and-seek, or staged epic girls versus boys battles, our days were filled with joy and mischief.

One of our favorite places to play was Talal's room. Located on the third floor of Grandpa's big house, it felt like a magical kingdom designed just for kids. The floor was covered in fake green grass, turning the room into an indoor playground. A massive chalkboard stretched across one wall, and we spent hours pretending to be in school. Sara and I would play the role of stern teachers, while Yasser and Talal were the unruly students causing chaos in the imaginary classroom.

The centerpiece of Talal's room was his life-sized race car bed. To us, it wasn't just a bed—it was a portal to adventure. We'd pile onto it, bounce on the mattress, and pretend we were speeding down imaginary highways, wind in our hair, laughter filling the air.

"*Who's the fastest driver?*" Yasser would yell, his voice full of excitement.

One day, during one of our chaotic race car adventures, Yasser started teasing Sara about her weight in the silly, mean-spirited way little brothers sometimes do. I wanted to stand up for Sara but couldn't stop laughing at Yasser's ridiculous jokes.

Sara turned bright red with frustration, tears welling in her eyes as she yelled at Yasser. Talal, meanwhile, sat frozen, his expression torn between wanting to laugh along with Yasser and feeling awful for Sara's hurt feelings.

Even then, at such a young age, Talal's empathy and emotional sensitivity were clear.

Looking back, I realize moments like these captured the essence of our childhood—innocent chaos, playful teasing, and an unspoken loyalty that bound us together. No matter how many water balloons were thrown, pranks pulled, or teasing words exchanged, the bond between the four of us was unbreakable.

We weren't just relatives, siblings, or friends in those fleeting, joy-filled days. We were a little tribe ruling over a race car bed kingdom and building memories that would stay with us forever.

· · · ● · ● ● · ·

Talal was the most spoiled one of us. He was the baby of the family, and there was a huge age gap between him and his older siblings, who lived at Grandpa's. Since his mother wasn't around, Grandpa overcompensated by giving Talal extra special treatment.

Anytime Talal so much as whimpered, everyone would come running. *"What's wrong? What happened?"* they'd fuss overprotectively. I can still picture him bawling his eyes out after the smallest squabble or teasing comment from us. Talal would go running to find his dad, crying like we had committed some horrible injustice against him.

It was enough to set off Talal's tears even when it was just a typical kid conflict, like Sara pulling his hair or Yasser saying something mean. Being much more mature, his older sisters seemed to understand that this was just Talal working his baby charm for attention.

From the moment we first met little Talal, it was clear he shared an incredibly strong bond with his dad—a bond like no other. My dad vividly recalled that first encounter at Grandpa's house. Grandpa had called urgently, saying, *"Talal won't stop crying, and I must leave for work. Come quickly!"*

When we arrived, Talal was wailing inconsolably, big tears streaming down his tiny freckled cheeks. My dad said he felt sad watching Talal's utter devastation at his father's departure. To that little boy, his dad meant absolutely everything.

My dad tried gently comforting Talal, *"Your daddy will come back,"* but the sobbing just went on and on. Talal wanted his daddy and nobody else. It was like his whole world had been ripped away.

Finally, after what felt like forever, the rest of us kids managed to distract Talal with games and goofing around. Slowly, his cries turned to laughter as we played. But that initial, raw heartbreak had been so visceral.

In Talal's young mind, his father was his one constant—his mother, protector, and universe. Even briefly, the thought of being separated from that parental love shattered Talal's sense of safety and security.

I'll never forget witnessing the intense, primal bond between a son and his father from that day until the end. It was unconditional, beautiful, and gut-wrenching all at once.

· · · ● · ● ● · · ·

After my family moved from Riyadh to Khobar, I didn't see Talal as often as we used to. It was mostly occasional visits on weekends or holidays like Eid when our huge family would gather together. But even with the distance, Talal and I managed to stay pretty close as we grew older into our teenage years.

As Talal grew older, he faced the complexities of adolescence in a conservative environment. He wrestled with balancing strict cultural and religious rules with natural teenage curiosities, like developing a fondness for certain girls from a distance. Part of him craved spiritual freedom, but another felt shame for questioning what he had been taught.

Watching Talal navigate that inner tug-of-war during our turbulent teen years was fascinating. I admired how thoughtful and self-aware he was, even when grappling with tough questions most kids avoided.

There were so many rules about what was allowed and what was forbidden. Even just looking at a girl was considered wrong and off-limits. With such an incredibly conservative culture surrounding him, Talal felt constantly conflicted about desires that arose as he got older.

As a teenager, you start questioning who you are and what you believe in. But for Talal, that journey of self-discovery was extra complicated. His roots were a unique blend—half German-French, half Saudi. His very traditional Saudi father and German stepmother raised him in a deeply religious Muslim household. So, anytime Talal experienced normal teenage curiosities and crushes, he immediately felt guilty, as if he was doing something unforgivable.

I could see the struggle on his face as he admitted feeling attracted to them. Part of him knew those feelings were natural, but shame and fear would quickly creep in. *"This is wrong; I shouldn't be thinking these things,"* Talal would lament, worry etched across his face.

When I tried reassuring him by gushing about my teenage crushes, he'd suddenly snap into a stern, conservative lecture mode. *"You shouldn't be thinking like that either. It's not right,"* he'd scold, his face serious and his tone firm.

It was so confusing for both of us to navigate. One moment, we were two giddy, giggling teens reveling in our harmless puppy-love infatuations. The next, Talal morphed into a disapproving brother figure, chastising me for having impure thoughts. Straddling two opposing cultural identities, each insisted he pick a side and stick to their rules.

Then, around 15 years old, Talal's personality changed completely. He suddenly became very mature. Yes, he was more responsible in many ways, but he had also become conservative and strict, especially with rules and beliefs.

I was 17 then and had just started nursing college, living at their house. Oma (the German word for grandmother), Ursula, Sara, Yusra, and Talal lived there then. Returning to the childhood house with my childhood friends was a wonderful experience.

I was blessed that year with the best memories of Talal. I watched him grow and talk about his strawberry bushes, beautifully placed outside his bedroom window. I patiently waited for the first flower bud because that only meant a strawberry was being born.

We shared a love of collecting antiques. He was a coin collector, and I was a stamp collector. Going through the albums and getting a history lecture from him about every coin he owned felt boring then, but now, those memories fill my heart with joy.

We fought a lot, though. I was not as conservative as he was, but he was very conservative and protective. At that time, Talal no longer saw me as a friend. He saw himself as more like a guardian. He felt he needed to protect me from the outside world.

We were always told girls are like lollipops; if not wrapped and covered, flies and bugs would eat us. Talal took those lessons to heart.

I remember talking on the phone with my father one night. *"Who are you talking to?"* Talal asked.

"None of your business," the rebel in me said, wanting to protect my privacy and freedom.

I had never seen Talal so angry. His face turned bright red, filled with frustration. I went to my room and locked my bedroom door so he couldn't come in. But Talal started banging hard on the door, making a hole in it!

Finally, I unlocked the door, and Talal barged in. We started yelling at each other loudly, our voices echoing down the hallway.

I was so furious at Talal that night. I wanted to hurt his feelings as badly as he had hurt mine, so I said something mean about his mother, using a curse word I knew would cut deep.

It worked. Talal instantly burst into tears when I insulted his precious mom.

I knew how much Talal loved his mother. They talked on the phone frequently, and he held her in the highest regard. During Talal's spiritual development, he was often worried because his mom and half-sister were not Muslim.

"Do you think my mom and sister will go to heaven?" he would ask me with deep worry in his eyes.

"Are your mom and sister good people who don't steal or hurt others? If they're good humans, then of course they'll go to heaven! It doesn't just depend on their religion," I'd reassure him.

But Talal was stuck on what he had been taught—that anyone who wasn't Muslim would definitely go to hell, no questions asked.

On the night of our massive fight, I crossed a line with my words. The look of betrayal on Talal's tear-streaked face remains etched in my memory.

Finally, Grandpa came and settled the fight between us. But I'll never forget Talal's pained, shocked look after I said those cruel words.

It was an awful thing to say, and I regretted it immediately.

· · · · ● · ● · · ·

Since we were children, Talal dreamed of becoming a doctor like his father, who owned a huge hospital in Riyadh. It seemed like Talal's destiny. None of our other aunts, uncles, or Talal's siblings chose that path, though. They mostly pursued careers in healthcare but not in medicine specifically.

My mother is a psychologist, Aunt Dina is a speech therapist, and Aunt Maysa has a doctorate in psychology. My uncle Sarry earned a master's degree in healthcare administration and managed the business side of my grandfather's hospital. Sara and I both became nurses.

I always sensed Grandfather's quiet disappointment about that. When I told him during college applications that I wanted to be a nurse, his frown said it all: *"Shouldn't you become a doctor instead?"* I felt his hope weigh on me, but I laughed it off.

Grandfather pinned all his dreams on Talal, hoping he would carry on the family legacy. Talal seemed driven back then, too.

Each summer break, we eagerly worked as volunteers at Grandfather's hospital. We started in the file room, meticulously organizing endless stacks of patient records. But I lived for my shifts on the wards. Watching nurses gently tend to patients, I envisioned myself in that role, and my heart was filled with purpose.

"One day, that will be me," I'd whisper with determination. Talal seemed to share that same fire in his eyes back then. Looking back now, though, I can't help but wonder if I was projecting my passion onto him.

Sara and I both studied to be nurses, but Talal dreamed of becoming a doctor. After finishing high school, he attended college for his first year and studied medicine. He wanted to be a surgeon when he started medical school! Talal didn't want any special favors just because his father owned a hospital. *"I want to earn it. I want to deserve it,"* he'd say with quiet determination.

When Talal turned 17, he moved from Riyadh to Khobar to attend medical school. That was the same year my parents got divorced. My mom had her own house, so Talal would often come over. He and my brother Yasser were inseparable that whole year.

Talal and I even went to the same university in Khobar. I was studying to become a nurse while he was in the medical program to become a doctor. Talal was just two years younger than me. I had already started my hospital training that year.

I was looking forward to the day Talal would begin his hospital rotations. I imagined us passing each other in the hospital hallways, sharing quick smiles between shifts. But sadly, that never happened because of what occurred later that year.

Over time, Talal began to question whether medicine was truly his calling. He thought about possibly taking over the family business at his dad's hospital instead. Talal had goals of running the business side, too.

It's strange to think about now—how those dreams and conversations were cut so tragically short.

· · · ● · ● ● · ·

When Talal moved to Khobar for his studies, the three of us—Talal, Yasser, and I—spent most of our time at my mom's or Aunt Dina's house. Aunt Dina lived in a nice compound with a pretty front yard area. She had two benches outside where we'd all sit and talk for hours.

We all secretly smoked cigarettes back then, even though we tried to hide it from each other. One by one, we'd sneak away for a quick smoke, pretending no one noticed. But of course, we all knew exactly what was going on.

Talal and I often went on long car rides together. I'd hop in his car and drive around aimlessly as he showed me different houses he liked or places he dreamed of living one day. Those carefree cruises gave us uninterrupted time to talk, dream, and confide in each other.

During one of our drives, Talal opened up to me. *"There's someone I feel connected to here in Khobar,"* he admitted shyly. Then he hesitated and added, *"And there's also someone else back in Riyadh."*

Talal was navigating emotional complexities in a conservative culture. On the one hand, he admired Nada, a girl from Riyadh who was extremely conservative and always fully covered. On the other hand, there was Shatha, a girl from the Aramco community nearby, who was open-minded, modern, and full of life.

I listened as Talal poured his heart out about these two girls, and I did my best to offer advice without judgment. Talal was always so polite and decent, never crossing boundaries. Even in his affection, there was a deep sense of respect.

Our community hosted a grand play that summer, and I played one of the lead roles. The play lasted seven days, with two shows every day. Friends and family, including Talal, were all involved. Some acted in small roles, others sold tickets, and some worked behind the scenes. It was an unforgettable summer filled with creativity, laughter, and teamwork.

During those months, Talal and Shatha grew closer. Their bond was tender and youthful but also complicated. Shatha's playful and carefree nature balanced Talal's more reserved and introspective personality.

But their connection wasn't perfect. Talal would confide in me about the moments that hurt him—the times Shatha would seem distant or unclear in her feelings. Sometimes, she'd tell him she was in the hospital when he came to visit, only for him to find out she wasn't actually there.

"Why would she do that?" He'd ask me, his voice heavy with confusion and hurt.

I never had a clear answer for him. Teenage emotions are messy, unpredictable, and often unfair.

Years later, when I decided to write about Talal's life, I contacted Shatha. I wanted to understand her side of the story and hear her perspective on their connection and what it meant to her.

"Dalia, if I told the full story of my relationship with Talal, I would need many, many pages," she told me.

I asked her to share whatever she felt comfortable with, but I never received anything from her.

That same year, I got engaged to my first fiancé, Mahir. He was a doctor who loved playing the guitar, and he and Talal hit it off immediately. Talal admired Mahir's open-mindedness, his kindness, and his romantic spirit.

"He's so cool, Dalia. I want to be like him someday." Talal once told me with a smile.

They bonded over their love for music and even shared a preference for the same guitar brands.

During that time, my parents were finalizing their divorce, and I struggled with the emotional weight of it all. Talal became my anchor during those months. He would pick me up for long drives, let me vent, and offer gentle words of wisdom.

"You don't know what plans are in store," he'd say softly. *"But you have to believe they are good plans happening for a reason."*

When I eventually decided to end my engagement with Mahir, Talal was deeply disappointed. He had grown attached to Mahir and had envisioned him as a permanent part of our family.

Talal brought his guitar to my mom's house to cheer me up and spent hours teaching me simple chords. We'd sit together, and I would sing off-key while he patiently strummed.

One of our favorite songs was *"So Close, No Matter How Far"* by Metallica. Talal played it beautifully while I sang my heart out, processing my sadness and heartbreak through music.

Those late-night jam sessions with Talal became a refuge for me. They were moments of pure connection, laughter, and healing.

Looking back, I treasure those hours spent with Talal, two guitars in hand and hearts wide open.

• • • ● • ● • • •

Talal tried to teach us French. He could speak four languages: English, Arabic, German, and French. My friends and I suddenly decided we wanted to learn French, too, so we asked him to give us lessons.

We met at my Aunt May's house and set up a makeshift classroom in her basement. Talal was thrilled about his new role as our teacher. He came prepared: a whiteboard, colorful markers, neatly arranged desks, and stacks of notebooks and pens. Everything was set up perfectly, and his enthusiasm was contagious.

We sat down, trying to look serious, pencils in hand, ready to learn. Talal started teaching us about French vowels, pronunciation, and basic phrases. But within minutes, my friends and I exchanged puzzled looks. None of us had the slightest clue what he was talking about.

Talal's excitement faded as he realized we weren't as serious about learning as he was. His patience slowly gave way to frustration.

Later that evening, Talal called me. *"Why did you all give up so quickly?"* he asked, his voice tinged with disappointment.

Jokingly, I replied, *"We didn't! Deema and I can speak French now!"*

"What do you mean? How can you speak French already?" Talal asked, genuinely confused.

"Yeah, I call her and say, 'Bonjour, comment ça va?' And she says, 'Ça va bien.' See, we speak French!"

There was a brief pause on the line, and then we both burst into laughter.

Talal had poured so much care and dedication into those lessons, even when we weren't taking them seriously. Looking back, those moments remind me of his unwavering patience, earnest desire to share knowledge, and deep love for the people around him.

Losing him left a hole in our family that can never be filled. But I'll always carry the memory of Talal standing in front of that whiteboard, marker in hand, determined to teach us something new—no matter how much we resisted.

• • • ● • ● • ● • • •

Talal lived a beautiful tapestry of love, family, and tenacity. From his varied background to his relentless dedication to those in his care, he united everyone in a manner no one else could.

His ability to make others visible, appreciated, and understood was exceptional. Talal left a lasting impression on everyone he came across, whether by his soft words, friendly smile, or the way he would pluck his guitar and lose himself in the music.

His friendliness was modest, steady, and very sincere rather than loud or flashy. Beyond his years, he had great empathy and loved fiercely, safeguarding the people he cared about.

Losing him created an emptiness that was never satisfied by anything. No laughter will sound like his, no song will play quite the same way, and no discussion will convey the special mix of wit and sincerity he gave to every engagement.

But Talal's memory lives on in the countless lives he touched. It lives on in the lessons he left behind, the melodies he played, and the love he gave so freely.

On the hardest days, I remind myself, *"He's not truly gone. As long as we keep his memory alive, Talal will always be with us—in our stories, hearts, and quiet moments when we hear his favorite song playing in the background."*

His story isn't one of loss but of love—a love so powerful that it continues to shine even in his absence.

What I Miss Most
The Little Moments That Mean Everything

I f I could see Talal's face again, I'd tell him how much I loved him and hug him tight, never letting go. Talal was like an angel—kind and caring, with a special way of making everyone around him feel warm and happy. When he smiled, the whole room seemed to light up. I miss that smile so much. But he's gone forever. That thought tears me apart.

The memory of our last moments together still haunts me—the missed calls, the silent goodbyes, the moments I let slip away. I carry those regrets heavily, but I'm learning to forgive myself, knowing none of us live as if every moment is the last.

My family avoids talking about Talal now, but I can't stop thinking about him. To fill the silence, I reached out to his loved ones—friends and roommates—whose stories only deepened my appreciation of who Talal was. They all described him the same way: a brilliant, kind-hearted person who brought people together. Knowing the impact he had on so many lives comforts me, but it also makes the emptiness he left behind even more profound. I long to be part of that community that grieves him while celebrating his memory.

• • • ● • ● ● • • •

Sometimes, I long to see Talal again, even if only in a dream. I imagine telling him how much he meant to me, how he was more than an uncle—he was like a brother. I'd remind him that he'll always be my guardian angel, watching over us. And I'd plead for a sign, any small gesture to know he's still near. Anything to bridge the distance and feel connected to him once more.

Talal's memory is a mixed bag of sorrow and laughter. Whenever I talk about him, a flood of long-forgotten tales bursts back to occupy the void he left behind. Pain clouds my heart as I try to recollect the happy times we last spoke about. But when I came clean with Talal, those treasured memories returned like sunshine peeking through the clouds.

Talal was sometimes said to be quiet and peaceful, his pure and compassionate attitude exuding a nearly celestial presence. Still, one of his best friends called him brave, surprising me. This picture conflicted with the quiet, reticent Talal I knew. But I started to see as she told their story. Though close, their relationship encountered many difficulties. Even when she withdrew or kept her distance, Talal remained patient and steadfast, valuing their connection above all else.

Talal and this girl had a meaningful friendship that began when they were 12. Despite their youth, their connection was shaped by shared experiences and challenges. The girl often distanced herself, but Talal remained patient, valuing their bond and hoping to mend things. She lived far away in a different city, which made it hard for them to see each other.

But Talal never gave up, even when she kept walking away. That takes a lot of bravery for someone so shy!

Hearing these stories about Talal's courage and devotion to those he cared about revealed his new side to me. He had this inner strength and determination, especially regarding the people he cared about. That makes me love and miss him even more.

$$\bullet \ \bullet \ \bullet \ \bullet \ \bullet \ \bullet \ \bullet \ \bullet \ \bullet \ \bullet$$

Whenever I recall memories of Talal, my heart feels full and heavy. He was kind, thoughtful, and always there for his family. I'm grateful I got to know him so well and be his friend. Even though he's gone now, I'll never forget his beautiful mark on our lives.

One story, in particular, stood out to me. "*He's the one who kept reaching out,*" she told me, her voice full of wonder. "*And deep down, she knew he would.*" Talal was persistent and devoted, and he never lost his cool or got rude, even when his close friend didn't respond to his calls. Instead, he would politely talk to her dad, saying hi and that everything was fine.

The girl's friend once conveyed a humorous message: "*Talal says to respond, or he might sleep in your front yard on the grass until he gets an answer.*" At first, she didn't believe it. Sure enough, though, Talal was sleeping on the grass all night, resolved to convey his authenticity and dedication.

• • • • • • • • • • •

Reading about these tales let me see Talal from another aspect. Benevolent in his demeanor, he possessed amazing inner strength and relentless determination. Romantic, ready to travel to tremendous distances for the ones he loved.

Talal is no more, yet his great heart and valiant spirit endure. His narrative reminds me of the need for true love in a society too frequently focused on being cool and pragmatic. Talal taught me it's worth fighting for what matters, no matter how hard it gets.

On one hand, I love hearing stories that reveal new sides of him. But on the other, it's a painful reminder that he's gone. There's one thing, in particular, that I regret—a fight we had where I said something awful to hurt him.

I can still picture Talal's face so clearly. When I cussed out his mom, his expression shifted, and his cheeks flushed red. Tears were in his eyes, and I could tell he felt so betrayed. I knew better than anyone how strong Talal's bond was with his mom. I knew how much he loved and missed her. And I'm sure he saw in my face that I only said those hurtful things to wound him deeply. Thinking about that memory still makes me cringe. If I could talk to Talal again, I would say, "*I'm so sorry. Please forgive me. Thank you for 19 years of friendship, and I love you.*"

• • • ● • ● • • •

What I miss most about Talal is a combination of his smile and his eyes. He had these deep, expressive eyes that seemed to reveal everything he was feeling. No matter what, Talal could never hide his emotions—you could always read them in his eyes. I remember how his eyes would get that naughty, *"Oh no, I got caught!"* look when I'd give him a certain look. He'd smile slightly like he knew he couldn't fool me. I loved that playful side of him.

I will always treasure those subtle gestures and expressions that set Talal apart, even if he is no more. Closing my eyes helps me see his face clearly, inspiring a mixed-fevers smile on mine. I will always carry the love and fun we experienced.

• • • ● • ● • • •

Coming to terms with the past twenty years hasn't been easy, especially with how unforgiving I've been toward myself. My deepest regret is not answering Talal's call and missing the chance to say a proper goodbye. I know why he called that day—I can almost hear what he wanted to say. But I chose not to answer. That decision remains one of the most heartbreaking aspects of this loss.

The last two times I saw Talal, I didn't get to say goodbye properly. I was on the phone the first time and didn't notice him walking away. I just heard his voice and saw him from behind as he left. I could have called or waved goodbye to him, but I didn't. Then, he called me the next time, but I didn't pick up. I missed my chance to talk to him one last time.

When I finally shared this with my mom a few months ago, her words stayed with me: "*You don't live with people like it's the last time you'll see them. That's not how life works.*" She was right—no one can predict those final moments. I shouldn't blame myself for not giving Talal the kind of goodbye he deserved. I was living in the moment, unaware it would be our last. Still, the weight of those lost possibilities hangs. Often, the guilt has overwhelmed my capacity to truly honor the happiness he brought into my life or grieve him. One continuous, tenacious friend on this road has been self-blame.

But I know I need to heal from this. I can't carry this guilt around forever. It's preventing me from honoring Talal's memory in the way he deserves. He was such an amazing friend, and I want to focus on celebrating the 19 years we had together rather than beating myself up over the end.

· · · ● · ● · · ·

If I could rewrite that moment, I know what I would say to Talal on the call, and I regret not answering. I'd begin with an apology: "*Hi, Talal. I'm so sorry I didn't pick up. I've been busy,*" even though that wasn't the truth—I was avoiding the call for reasons I didn't fully understand at the time. Then I'd ask, "*What's on your mind?*" I can almost hear his kind, worried voice on the other end, gently asking how I was holding up. The truth is, I wasn't. My parents were divorcing, my dad was remarrying, and I had just ended my engagement. My world felt like it was unraveling around me.

Normally, I tend to keep my feelings bottled up and pretend I'm okay. But with Talal, I know I would have opened up. I would have probably told him, "*I'm not okay. I'm struggling with all the problems at home.*"

Talal had a remarkable ability to bring calm into chaos. Despite being younger than me, his words carried wisdom far beyond his years. Whenever everything in my life felt like it was falling apart, he was the one I could turn to. I can still picture him saying, with his steady, comforting voice, "*This too shall pass. Hard times don't last forever. Have faith—with every difficulty comes ease.*"

Had only I paid attention to that call. One last time, hearing his voice might have provided the solace I now so sorely need. The way the discussion would have gone—his subdued voice inquiring how I was doing and providing his usual words of encouragement—almost seems clear. But I didn't answer, and soon after, he was gone. The thought still haunts me; he was always there for me, yet I failed to be there for him in his final moments.

· · · · ●· ● · · ·

Dreams have evolved into a comforting and guiding tool, a link between Talal and me. He calmly looked at me in one especially vivid dream and said, "*Dalia, I am okay. I want you to be good.*" Those words felt like a reassurance from beyond, a message of peace that settled deep within me.

Another dream felt like a window into heaven itself. I ascended a stair to reach a rooftop bathed in radiant light, where Talal awaited. Emotionally overwhelmed, I rushed to him, holding him tightly, letting my love and longing pour forth. As I clung to him, he gently opened a door to a place filled with light and greenery. He began to step through but stopped me, pushing me back and closing the door. I knew then that he was telling me it wasn't my time—I still had a life to live. But his presence and peace reassured me that he was in a good place.

From that moment, I started to feel his warm, guiding presence in different ways. The first time was during my college graduation—I saw Talal walking beside me as I crossed the stage. It was as though he was still there, witnessing life's milestones with me.

Later, in a profound moment of meditation, I felt him again. His presence was so vivid, his voice so clear—*"I am okay, and I want you to be okay."* This moment came when I was beginning to truly grieve his loss, and it felt like a divine whisper nudging me toward healing.

Along this journey, I have come to witness God's hand in the many ways He speaks—through dreams, spiritual experiences, and the stories of those who loved Talal. Every memory, every sign, feels like a supernatural whisper, gently guiding me through the waves of grief. My faith has deepened over time, and I now see people as vessels for heavenly messages, offering comfort and insight exactly when needed.

· · · ● · ● · · ·

While guilt over missing Talal's last call lingered for a long time, I eventually realized that holding onto that regret would only keep me from healing. Slowly, I found comfort in the goals I set for myself—they became stepping stones on my path to recovery.

Now, I see Talal's soul as a lighthouse, softly pushing me to treasure our lovely memories instead of lamenting over his absence. He was really one of a kind—a close friend whose words might help me, even in my worst hours.

He was always there to listen without judgment and had such a grown-up, peaceful demeanor. I can hear his comforting voice saying to me, *"It will pass. The difficult times will not always last. Have trust; easy will follow from struggle,"* even now, he is gone.

I'm glad I spent time with Talal, even if the hole in my heart may never completely heal. His generosity, knowledge, and unflinching support have permanently changed my life. And through these mystical experiences, I know he's still looking out for me every step of the way. Talal may be physically gone, but his spirit lives on. Whenever I need strength or guidance, I can feel his presence. He was—and always will be—an angel watching over me.

· · · ● · ● · · ·

When I consider how I wish Talal to be remembered, the term *"angel"* arises right away. Touching everyone in his vicinity, he personified pure, unqualified love. At just 19 years old, Talal left such a lasting and significant influence on so many people—quite amazing. Talal had a remarkable ability to make everyone feel appreciated and cared for—from his family to friends to even casual acquaintances. Always there, he gave anyone in need his unflinching support regardless of the situation.

Incredibly, he found time to be deeply connected with so many people, especially considering he spent the first few years of his life living with his mother. Every person I spoke with who knew him bonded with him differently but equally powerfully. Talal and his compassionate treatment touched his friends, my father, aunts, and cousins very personally.

One of my cousins even wrote a heartfelt poem about Talal titled *Absolute Love*. I couldn't agree more when he shared it with me—it perfectly encapsulated Talal's essence as a source of pure, unconditional love. The poem felt like a tribute that truly did him justice. The simple truth is that Talal was deeply loved by everyone who knew him. Something so angelic and special about him drew people in and made them feel safe, accepted, and cared for. Even in his short 19 years, he left an indelible mark on many lives.

• • • ● • ● • • •

Thinking about Talal, I'm always amazed by how selflessly he gave of himself to others. Always there, he provided a listening ear and consistent encouragement. Most importantly, he had the ability to schedule the time and effort needed to affect so many lives so profoundly. When I consider Talal's life, one of the most poignant tales comes from a close buddy, he much loved in his earlier years. She described Talal as someone too pure and innocent for the harshness of this world, believing that his gentleness and goodness were why he was taken from us so soon.

His loyalty and kindness never faltered. She explained that Talal would never angrily end the call, even when she turned him down. Instead, he would always talk politely because, in his innocent heart, he could never imagine doing anything wrong to anyone.

She shared a particularly funny story when Talal slept on the grass outside her house all night to get her attention. He was so determined to reach her that he wouldn't leave until she answered. It's such a vivid, hilarious image—this sweet, gentle boy refusing to give up, no matter what.

Despite their difficulties, Talal's close friend told me how strongly bonded she felt to him. She called her time with him the *"innocent part"* of her life, noting that even while she finds thinking about him difficult, it makes her smile. She was permanently changed by his pure, unwavering devotion.

Hearing these tales from a close friend of Talal changed my respect for his character. Even if others may have behaved cruelly, he really saw the best in others and presumed the most benign intentions. Talal was as charming as she was sad; she had a wide-eyed awe about the world. The facts of reality did not always line up with his soft, trusting demeanor. Perhaps that's what made him so unique, though—he refused to allow the challenges around him to reduce his capacity for love and compassion.

• • • ● • ● • • •

One of my most cherished memories of Talal is how he would sit with me and patiently teach me to play the guitar. Hearing one of his close friends describe those moments together brought back a strong sense of déjà vu. It's amazing to me how Talal was able to connect with so many people in such a deep, meaningful way.

Talal's roommate also told me about him, describing him as an *"angel"*—someone incredibly calm, mature, and wise beyond his years. My mother even called him a *"healer,"* saying she keeps one of his belongings in a sacred place in her therapy room because it reminds her of his special, soothing presence.

What I loved most about Talal was how truly present he was, no matter who he was with. Whether it was with me, his first love, or anyone else, he gave them his full attention and focus. He wasn't distracted by phones or other things—when he was with you, he was there, at that moment, listening intently and sharing from the heart.

Talal had such a deep, authentic spirituality. While I grew up fearing God, Talal loved Him with all his heart. It was refreshing to hear Talal's perspective on faith and connect with him over those meaningful conversations.

If I could go back in time and know that Talal's life would be cut short, I wouldn't change a thing about the time we spent together. Every moment we shared was precious because he was present and engaged. What I miss most about Talal are the little things—his warm eyes, gentle smile, and ability to elevate any conversation into a profound, spiritual discussion.

He had this incredible ability to make you feel seen, heard, and valued, no matter who you were.

• • • ● • ● • • •

Talal's unconditional love and unwavering presence made him so special. He gave himself completely to each relationship, whether with me or someone else. He had a way of making each person feel like the most important one in his life. As I've been connecting with the people who loved Talal the most, I've realized that the healing process doesn't have to be painfully difficult every time we think about him.

There have been moments when talking about Talal that have brought me a genuine smile, especially when I hear the stories and insights shared by those closest to him. So many people I've spoken to have poured their hearts out, sharing their cherished memories and Talal's profound impact on their lives.

Hearing their perspectives has been both heartbreaking and uplifting. Because the emotions can be overwhelming, I've had to limit my conversations to about half an hour. One of Talal's close friends, in particular, has been able to talk for hours about their time together.

Whenever I have to end our chats, I apologize and tell her, *"I know, I know—I would love to listen for hours, but I'm just not ready for that yet. Let me process this, and we'll talk again soon."*

I also looked forward to connecting with another relative who had a close bond with Talal. I was supposed to meet with her, but we agreed to have a phone call instead. From what I understand, she's the one who's pushed herself through the grieving process, even going on her honeymoon to visit Talal's mother and connect with her.

Through these conversations, it's clear that Talal left an indelible mark on many lives. While the pain of his loss will always be present, there's also a profound sense of gratitude and joy in being able to celebrate his legacy. The people who loved him the most find healing and comfort in coming together and sharing their stories.

• • • ● • ● • • •

I found an old magazine from 35 years ago. The cover had a crazy headline: *"Saudi Millionaire Kidnaps His Own Son!"* My heart skipped a beat when I realized it was about my grandfather and Talal.

I had always known Talal's story differed slightly from the rest of us. He wasn't just my uncle—Talal was more like a brother to me. But as I read that magazine, I learned the heartbreaking truth behind how he ended up living with our family.

My grandfather took him away from his mother when Talal was a tiny baby. It was like something out of a movie—Talal's mom tried to fight it, even getting Interpol involved. But in the end, my grandfather managed to keep Talal and raise him here with us.

I can't imagine how scary and sad that must have been for Talal's poor mom. One day, she was cuddling her baby, and the next, he was gone without a trace. My mom had a similar story—when she was little, my grandfather had also taken her away from her mother. But at least Grandma willingly handed my mom over. Talal's mom had no choice at all.

As a kid, I remember traveling with Talal's family to countries like Syria and Egypt. That was the only way his mom could see him since she couldn't come to our house in Saudi Arabia without my grandfather getting in trouble. I felt so bad for Talal. He was just a child but was being used as a pawn in this grown-up battle.

Even though Talal was ripped away from his mom at such a young age, he was still super close to his dad. My grandfather spoiled him rotten, and Talal adored him. I don't think he even realized at first that he'd been taken away against his will.

But as Talal got older, I could see him struggling with all these mixed-up feelings. One summer, after visiting his mom in Germany, he returned upset. Talal told me his mom had introduced him to some new man she was dating, and he didn't like it.

Deep down, Talal knew that the whole situation with his mom was messed up. But he was still just a teenager, not even 20 years old. If Talal had lived longer, I bet he would have started to unpack all that childhood trauma of being taken from his mother. It must have been so confusing and painful.

Talal never openly shared his feelings about being taken away. Despite everything, he seemed to hold no anger towards his father. He loved his father so much, even though what Grandpa did was wrong. I wonder if Talal was scared to question it or if he had buried those feelings so deeply that he didn't even know they were there.

· · · ● · ● · · ·

Whenever I think about Talal's story, my heart aches. He deserved so much better than having his own family rip him away from the woman who gave birth to him. That's the kind of thing that can scar a person for life.

Though Talal didn't live to see his 20th birthday, I believe the trauma of being taken from his mother would have continued to haunt him throughout his life. How could it not? Imagine being a baby, safe and warm in your mother's arms one day, and then suddenly waking up with strangers in a strange new house. That's the kind of thing nightmares are made of.

Sometimes, I wonder if Talal and his mom could have rebuilt their bond had they reunited as adults—or if the pain of their past would have been too overwhelming. Not knowing is one of the hardest parts.

· • • • • • • • • • ·

Talal deserved so much more than the hand life dealt him. He was a kind, loving person—the glue that held our crazy family together. He was like a big brother to all of us. He embraced us as his family and made sure we always felt it.

Reflecting on Talal's story, I'm reminded of the harsh truth that life often isn't fair. Bad things often happen to the best people, and we can do little to change it. But Talal never let the darkness of his past define him. He just kept shining his beautiful light, bringing joy to everyone around him until the end.

I wish Talal could have had the chance to work through all that trauma, to finally be reunited with his mom and heal those deep wounds. But at least he knew he was loved, even if it wasn't by the one person who should have loved him most. Although Talal was taken from his mom as a baby, he always found a home with us.

The Things People Say
Finding Sweet Moments in Sorrow

Thinking back to Talal's funeral fills me with a strange, unsettled feeling. There were two separate services: one in Riyadh, where he lived, and another in Khobar, where our family was based. My memories of the Riyadh funeral are blurry—just fragmented images of that overwhelming day.

At the funeral, I saw my cousin Nada. She and Talal had shared a deep bond during their teenage years. After the accident, I broke the devastating news to her—something I only fully remembered later when she reminded me.

She recounted how she had called my aunt Yusra's phone, and I was the one who answered. Expecting a laid-back conversation, Nada greeted me but sensed something in my unsteady voice right away.

"Nada, I need to tell you something. Please stay calm," I quietly urged.

"What? What's going on?" she asked, her voice rising with panic.

I took a deep breath. *"You need to be calm,"* I repeated gently, hearing her steadying breaths on the other end.

With my heart pounding, I said the hardest words I've ever had to say: *"Nada... Talal was in a car accident. He didn't make it. I'm so sorry."*

Silence followed. She couldn't speak, and then she began sobbing uncontrollably. Nada said she may have even dropped the phone in shock and heartbreak.

I don't recall that phone call myself. Nada later told me she sought me out at the funeral because, despite the life-shattering news, I had sounded peaceful and compassionate.

· · · · · ● · ● · · · ·

Even years later, I still choke up, reliving those final moments with Talal—saying goodbye at two somber funerals and grappling with the permanence and unfairness of his loss. The truth is, I was a total wreck inside—devastated beyond words.

In those first few horrible days and weeks after Talal's sudden death, it felt like I was going through the motions, grieving my sweet uncle-brother-best friend, who was taken from us way too soon. So young, with an amazing life ahead of him, Talal would never get to experience the future he deserved. The agony of losing him was unbearable for me and everyone who loved him.

I'll never forget shattering Nada's world with tragic news no young person should ever have to hear. On the outside, I kept cool; on the inside, I was disintegrating. I stammered through ordinary chores and contacts in a numbing, grief-stricken fog, keeping my composure by a thread.

Often, I wonder how Talal's life may have turned out if he were still alive. What type of friend, parent, or husband would he have developed? Still imprinted in my memory are his early innocence and his relationship with Nada on that fateful night, a moving reminder of all that was lost.

The days after Talal's accident passed in a cloud of extreme grief. I was numb, grappling with the shocking finality of his loss.

I remember sitting in the room, feeling hollowed out inside. Talal's sister Sara, who, given our close age, feels more like a peer to me, approached me during one of those somber moments. Tears flooded her face as Sara gave me a shaking hug. Her tears reflect the same shared suffering we experienced. I froze, unable to call forth my own tears while she sobbed. I was numb to the tremendous loss all around us and emotionally spent.

· · · · ● · ● · · ·

Following Talal's accident, a wave of anger consumed me. I was furious at how suddenly he was taken from us, how unfairly life had ripped him away without any warning. The sheer injustice of it made me want to scream.

Denying Talal's accident became my coping strategy right away. I imagined him straying the desert—alive but lost—in illogical situations. I grabbed at fervent prayers, hoping this dream was only a nasty error. Still, denial crumbled and gave way to a deep, all-consuming frustration as the days went by.

I resisted the sadness that grief brought because surrendering to it would mean confronting the unbearable truth that Talal was gone forever. Allowing myself to feel sadness would have made his loss undeniable—a reality I wasn't yet ready to face.

Rather, I trapped myself in a loop of rage—rejecting tears, turning away from any consolation given, and separating myself from the collective grief of my family. My fury at the planet turned into a shield, a safer release than facing the terrible reality of his absence.

My mother nearly had to drag me downstairs to eat as I had lost all appetite. Sitting at the table, absentmindedly picking at my food, I overheard two women whispering nearby. *"Such a tragedy,"* one murmured, shaking her head. *"May God rest his soul. He was such a smart, good boy for his age."* Their words ignited a fire within me. Who were these strangers to talk about Talal as though they truly knew him? The thought made my face flush with anger. How dare they publicly mourn him without understanding who he truly was? I scowled at them, my anger boiling under the surface as I pushed myself to eat.

They hardly deserved to say his name at all. The wrath swirled inside me, growing intolerable, until I eventually bolted away, leaving my plate untouched. For a long time following the funeral, I remained consumed by a state of simmering resentment and fury.

• • • ● • ● • • •

Looking back, I see now that my anger was an immature defense mechanism—a way to shield myself from vulnerability, to avoid confronting the overwhelming pain of loss. Anger felt safer, more manageable, than accepting the devastating reality of Talal's permanent absence.

In the days following Talal's accident, I felt like an exposed nerve—raw, hypersensitive, and vulnerable. Even the faintest whisper could ignite my simmering anger and pain. I remember someone whispering, *"Poor Talal's father...how will he cope with this tragedy?"* Their remarks set up a white-hot explosion of wrath in me. These people were to be my uncle's mourners? Unlike me, they knew him not at all! I seethed in my mind: *"Keep silent and go if you are here at the funeral. Nobody calls for your fake sympathies."*

Deep down, I knew my rage was illogical, yet I couldn't stop myself from excluding everyone. When I was still drowning in my own, it seemed difficult to accept their sorrow. Actually, I have always felt quite awkward at funerals and memorials.

I remember the funeral at my grandfather's house. He was lying on a couch while mourners filtered past, briefly kissing his head. The entire scene felt so impersonal, so unsettling. In those initial shock-filled days of grieving Talal, I craved solitude. Even polite murmurs of sympathy felt unbearable, each interaction dredging up raw, unprocessed pain.

My anger became a defensive wall, shielding me from the vulnerability of my sadness and keeping the raw grief at bay.

I've always felt a deep discomfort at traditional funeral services, a feeling that's lingered since childhood. I remember attending one for a woman who had passed away. Her mother, still alive, lay motionless on a couch, seemingly disconnected from everything around her. Visitors would sit briefly before the grieving mother, mumble their condolences, and shuffle away without lingering. But she seemed unaware of their presence, lost in her own world. I couldn't help but wonder—why force her to endure this ritual in such a fragile state?

At that same funeral, I remember the woman's daughter sitting alone in an upstairs room. Yet someone fetched her, insisting she rejoin the gathering downstairs, even though she likely longed for privacy. It struck me as deeply inconsiderate to force her into public mourning when she clearly needed solitude.

That's why I appreciated how funerals were handled during COVID—smaller, more intimate remote gatherings. An online memorial page allowed people to leave a simple 'rest in peace' message and quietly exit without the weight of prolonged ceremonies. For me, minimizing rituals and reducing the emotional strain of prolonged ceremonies feels far more humane.

· · · ● · ● ● · · ·

After Talal's tragic accident, being surrounded by a sea of acquaintances and distant relatives felt utterly overwhelming. People I barely knew offered overblown sentiments about Talal—words that felt hollow and disconnected, only deepening my sense of anger and alienation.

In those first days of shocked grief, I just wanted my closest relatives here. Only they could allow room for my frailty, free from sympathy or judgment. They allowed me time to freely negotiate the rawness of my emotions in those delicate, suspended periods of loss.

We all battled to negotiate the weight of our shared grief, so I tried to help the ones closest to Talal. Later, Nada told me how much it meant when I hugged her hard at the burial and whispered, *"I love you very much."* She had a close relationship with Talal. She said those basic words carried her across the first waves of pain. I recall holding Shatha, another person dear in Talal's life, close and softly coaxing her to glance at his image. She laid her head on my shoulder, and we watched as we seemed to be living an eternity. Shatha later confessed in me that her great comfort from the empty, agonizing agony came from our vulnerable time.

Fascinatingly, two persons very close to Talal in their own unique ways—Shatha and Nada—later sought comfort in each other's company while they mourned together. To me, this is a lovely picture: the two major loves of Talal's life discovering solace and resonance in their common heartbreak.

Talal's roommate, Farid, told me rather vividly that he and their other roommate couldn't think of returning to their flat without him. Simply too much to handle were the nothingness and Talal's residual echoes. Over those first terrible months, they leaned on one another for support and finally made the tough decision to move out together.

• • • ● • ● • • •

Early on, our family seemed to follow a pattern of quiet, lonely grieving. We bottled those deep feelings as though talking about them would help to make the terrible reality even more intolerable.

Looking back, I wish we had relied more on one another—had those difficult, awkward talks and let our common loss provide strength. Rather, we each withdrew into our own worlds of grief, bearing the terrible weight of losing Talal's vivid spirit—snapped away from us too soon.

Though I yearned for Talal's closest loved ones, I now see that maybe allowing room for each of our unique grieving paths was, in some sense, essential. This past year, I've been on a deeply personal journey—unpacking and gradually releasing the grief I had bottled up for so long after losing Talal. Reaching out to other family members, I've come to realize just how deeply many of them remain stuck in their mourning.

Whenever I attempt to open conversations about Talal and our shared grief, I'm often met with silence or an abrupt emotional shutdown. I might receive a terse sentence or two before they retreat again behind their emotional walls. Eventually, after multiple gentle attempts, some—like my father and Shatha—would briefly open up. Others, like Talal's sister Dina, could only offer the smallest crumbs of sharing before retreating inward again.

"It's just too painful to talk about him," she whispered, her eyes clouded with emotion. At that moment, I remembered how, not long ago, I, too, had been in that same self-protective space. If someone had pushed me to grieve openly just a year earlier, I know I would have frozen up, too.

The loss was too literal, too agonizing. I, therefore, do not criticize their ongoing guardedness—the instinct to keep those rusted, hardened layers of sadness firmly in place. Terrified of the deluge of emotions that might rush out, I can see the difficulty of tearing down such obstacles.

I can only establish a secure and vulnerable environment where I gently invite them to unburden their residual anguish beside me. Over this last year, I have come to see that loss is a complex interior experience with many levels to reveal rather than a single overpowering feeling. Beneath the great anguish of losing Talal lay other strong emotions I had long suppressed—feelings that begged to be felt and handled before I could really communicate my loss.

Resurfaced anger would bubble up unannounced. At first, it was a faint simmer—a useless wrath aimed outward at the terrible disaster of Talal. That fury changed inside over time to become a burning, self-directed rage. Shame, sorrow, and an aching sense of self-betrayal ate me. These bitter feelings surged over me in unrelenting waves of self-loathing and guilt.

The question *"Why?"* tormented me the most. Given such a terrible loss, *why was I so mercilessly punishing myself?* Traversing those emotional strata, terrible memories surfaced—moments I had missed, words I had omitted, and chances to convey how much I loved Talal. Regrets over my casual complacency in those final moments haunted me—never dreaming they would be our last.

I found myself replaying those small, seemingly inconsequential moments before the accident—each interaction becoming a source of angry self-reproach. I longed to turn back time and relive those fleeting moments with more presence and appreciation for Talal's irreplaceable presence. The weight of shame and remorse would, at times, feel utterly crippling.

My mother gently reminded me, *"We don't go about each day thinking this could be the last time we see someone. That's no way to live life."* She was right—I couldn't keep berating myself for something so unintentional, so deeply human. Though slowly, I eventually found my way to a delicate point of self-forgiveness.

I had to make peace with the fact that I hadn't realized just how precious those final moments with Talal truly were. And maybe that's okay—perhaps it was Talal's final gift to us: simply *being* together one last time without clinging or carrying the weight of looming farewells.

I've learned to let go of that inward anger, to stop punishing myself with endless *"what ifs"* and *"if onlys."* Instead, I've chosen to honor Talal's beautiful life by living more presently—cherishing every interaction, every shared moment, and every person's impact on my journey.

· • • ● • ● • • • ·

I've done the grueling work of healing my grief—allowing myself to revisit the pain as if his death had happened yesterday and truly letting myself feel every raw emotion. I know grief will always find ways to resurface—unannounced, uninvited, and often at the most unexpected moments. But I've found the courage to welcome it, sit with it, feel it fully, and gently let it pass through me.

Through this process, I've discovered something beautiful: the more I let go of the heaviness, the more the precious memories of Talal have come rushing back to me. The joyful times we spent felt buried under layers of darkness, wrath, and grief for so long. The weight of my suffering muffled and hid those happy memories—his grin, laughter, our unique link.

But as I have gently removed every defensive layer of grief and negativity, those happy times with Talal have started to surface, vivid and unambiguous. Little by little, I have begun to find reasons to smile once more when I think of him instead of being instantly depressed. Now, when I think back on a ridiculous inside joke we used, I start to smile rather than cry. Alternatively, a clear recall of his kind personality can flood me with warmth rather than guilt.

The heaviness has started to lift, creating space for light to shine through. Part of my struggle was the fear that if I stopped actively grieving Talal, it would mean I'd stop loving him or honoring his memory. I had clung so tightly to my grief, mistakenly believing it was the only connection I had left to him.

But now I understand—that isn't true at all. My grief doesn't define my love for Talal or make me who I am. It's the beautiful experiences and moments we shared that have shaped me—not the trauma of his passing. If anything, I dishonored both of us by staying trapped in that murky pool of endless mourning.

Sadness weighed on my soul, and instead of being lightened by the brilliant brightness Talal brought into my life. Indeed, his death has permanently changed my heart. But by really facing and working through my loss, I have been able to release the guilt and hurt, therefore allowing room for the great warmth and delight Talal brought into my life while he was still here.

My love for him hasn't diminished—it's grown alongside a deeper love and compassion for myself. By embracing this shift, I can now bask in the radiant glow of Talal's unforgettable presence rather than be consumed by the loneliness of his absence.

Being stuck in perpetual grief feels like being swallowed by an endless void of sorrow, consuming you from the inside out. But beneath that sadness lies a tangled web of other powerful emotions—anger, denial, shame, and resentment. Fear is at the core of it all, hovering like a shadowy undercurrent.

I've come to understand that fear is the root of all those turbulent and harmful emotions. Grief, at its essence, is an intense experience of fear—fear of loss, fear of change, fear of confronting those raw, messy emotions head-on. The most beautiful revelation I've had is that once I summoned the courage to face and heal that deep-rooted fear, true inner peace began to take place.

As fear's tight grip began to loosen, the darkness of deeply entrenched grief started to disperse—like clouds parting after a long storm. Finally, I could allow the positive, joyful memories and emotions to flow freely into that peaceful stillness. All the cherished little moments with Talal that once triggered intense heartache now bring warmth and even laughter.

I'm grateful to finally be finding peace around his death rather than being trapped in relentless anguish. I sometimes wish this clarity had come to me sooner—rather than two decades later. Perhaps I was too young before. Perhaps 40 carries a certain wisdom. Either way, I trust that everything unfolded as it was meant to.

Talal's radiant spirit was a profound gift to everyone who knew him. He had an incredible ability to turn even the most ordinary moments into something vibrant and meaningful simply by being fully present. When he directed his warm, dazzling smile toward you, it felt like you were the only person in the world who mattered.

That's why speaking his name has felt so painful over the years. Just hearing "*Talal*" would make many of us instinctively retreat, fearing that those beautiful memories would reopen the raw, aching wounds of our grief. Unhealed loss has been weighty and has kept many of us silent.

Still, something rather amazing started to happen as I traveled to find Talal's brilliant light. Bravely facing and organizing my own residual feelings over his death has helped others find the bravery and room to start their healing paths.

Many have gotten in touch to let me know how this memoir has unexpectedly cleared their road to healing around Talal's death. Some even admitted they had begun praying for him once more following years of quiet. Others have been going back over and honoring the cheeky, endearing tales that made Talal so wonderfully appealing. Our talks often turned into a mixed bag of intense, cathartic weeping and boisterous laughter. From belly-laughing at one of Talal's signature antics to crying over how much we miss his impish smile and glittering eyes.

Though they brought many emotions, everyone involved found great release when these memories surfaced and could be shared. Person after person has expressed gratitude: "*Thank you for this. I didn't realize how much unprocessed trauma I'd been carrying all these years. I feel so much lighter now.*" In those moments, I felt it, too—a gradual lifting of the heaviness, replaced by a newfound lightness of spirit.

I'm no longer running from the shadows of grief. Instead, I'm weaving them into the rich mosaic of Talal's extraordinary life and enduring legacy. Of course, grief still comes in waves, crashing over me when I least expect it. But I'm no longer drowning in it. I've learned to lean into the current—to feel, process, and let those emotions move through me without fearing their intensity.

That's why I've made a conscious effort to allow myself to fully feel and express those turbulent emotions as they arise instead of burying them deep inside. I now know to weep it out, talk it out, write it out—whatever it takes to let that pent-up energy come out.

I feel lighter and more at peace each time I stop, become present, and let myself cleanse those emotions. Though it still affects me, grief is no longer a stifling, motionless force dictating me. I have quit worrying about its weight.

Looking back, I realize that my greatest obstacle in processing Talal's loss was a deep-rooted fear of confronting those raw, messy emotions head-on. A fear of allowing myself to be vulnerable with the crippling sadness, the simmering anger, and the relentless waves of regret.

I was terrified of breaking down the emotional armor I'd carefully built as a shield. For so many of us—especially men—there's an unreasonable stigma around openly expressing painful emotions.

We're often told to bottle it up, to keep a brave face no matter how broken we feel inside. Tears or admissions of anguish are unfairly viewed as weakness or shameful displays of vulnerability.

But all that achieves is locking those raw, unprocessed emotions deep within your body, mind, and spirit—like shrapnel slowly poisoning you from the inside out. I have personally seen how unhealed sadness can harden and age even the nicest, warmest souls, transforming them into only ghosts of their former selves.

Many have seen how much lighter and more revitalized I seem this year as I started to release the emotional weight I have carried for so long. It's not just an internal shift; a visible rebirth happens when you let go of years of pent-up sorrow.

If I could offer advice from my journey, it would be this: allow yourself to feel and process raw emotions as they surface fully—don't numb or push them away. When that heavy weight settles on your chest, let it flow through you—cry, scream, or write—whatever releases that emotional burden.

Sometimes, I'll cry for what feels like an eternity, heaving with body-wracking sobs as memories and emotions pour out uncontrollably. It's agonizing at the moment, but afterward, there's a profound sense of lightness and clarity where that bottled anguish once festered.

I encourage anyone navigating grief to allow themselves to re-experience and express their emotions fully. *Think back—what happened when you lost your loved one? What do you miss the most about them?*

I gently lead them through those last hours and help them communicate whatever feelings surface. I reassure them that feeling everything—the hurt, the regrets, the anger—is safe. Not just courageous but also essential for actual healing is releasing those pent-up emotions through unfiltered, primal screams and shaking tears.

* * * * * * * * * *

Just weeks ago, a neighbor confided in me that she couldn't bring herself to enter her late father's favorite living room—it was too painful. When she returned home, I gently encouraged her to sit in his favorite recliner—to inhabit that sacred space, to feel his lingering presence. She later called me, her voice breaking with emotion, to tell how liberating and cathartic it had been to at last let those floodgates open.

Indeed, she let her anguish flow freely, sobbed, and lamented. But she discharged her anxiety about that place and its aura by doing this. The area seemed smaller, her wordless grief no more haunting.

Giving yourself complete permission to experience every component of your loss—no matter how raw or primal—has great power and rejuvenation. It's an act of bravery and healing to allow those feelings to escape the close confinement we try to force them into and cry with abandon.

Even now, when I think back to Talal's funeral, flashes of anger still resurface unexpectedly. I remember huddling in a corner with my friends, emotionally shutting everyone out.

I was jolted by the shock of laughter piercing through the heavy silence. I spotted one of my closest friends giggling with someone else over something trivial. In that moment, a white-hot surge of rage consumed me. How could she laugh—how could anyone laugh—at a time like this? It felt so insensitive, so deeply disrespectful.

I never confronted her about it, and even now, revisiting that memory stirs up a lingering resentment I can't fully shake.

Grief has a way of magnifying the smallest moments, turning them into irrational triggers for our pain and anger.

· · · ● ● · ● ● · ·

Another sharp memory from those first agonizing days is the conversation I had with my father about Talal's accident. My parents were newly divorced at the time, which somehow made delivering that horrific news even harder.

I called my dad, my voice flat and hollow as I numbly recited the facts: *"Talal was in a car accident. He didn't make it. I'm going to Riyadh with*

Mom and my siblings." My father jumped into his car with his new wife and began the long drive to Riyadh without hesitation.

He wanted to be there—for me, for all of us—to grieve Talal's loss together as a family. In the aftermath, I heard different accounts of how my father reacted during the funeral service. My uncle later told me he'd seen my normally stoic father *"sobbing like a child"* as he mourned over Talal's body.

The image of my father breaking down still makes my heart clench with a sudden wave of emotion. Despite the lingering rawness of his divorce, my father's love for Talal transcended every hurt and tension.

He chose to show up fully, bearing his anguish in front of my mother's entire family—a painful gathering made even more delicate by the lingering wounds of their split. And yet, he did it—out of immense love and respect for Talal's beautiful spirit.

I'll never forget the quiet dignity with which my father entered that space, where every wound was still raw and unhealed. He willingly entered a room filled with my mother's family and her father—people with whom he likely still held unresolved tensions. Yet, his presence alone spoke volumes about his profound love and connection for Talal.

Those first few days of shock and grief remain a hazy blur in my memory—a whirlwind of intense, swirling emotions that I've only started to unpack, layer by layer, years later.

Yet, when I reflect on my dad's actions during those fragile days, my heart swells with gratitude and love. His ability to set aside any lingering hurts or tensions from the divorce because honoring Talal's life was more important, more sacred, than anything else. Joining us all in our collective mourning, setting aside any unhealed anger or animosities for another day.

It was a poignant reminder that even in our most fractured and fragile emotional states, love has the power to heal, bridge divides, and create moments of connection.

My father carried that strength with him—an openness and vulnerability that shone brightly through the shared trauma our family endured.

As I continue to grapple with the tangled mix of emotions surrounding Talal's loss, my father's example inspires me to lean into love rather than be consumed by the heaviness of grief. To allow me to feel it all—the rawness, the ache—but to let the eternal bonds of love outshine the wounds, just as he did in those tender, vulnerable moments.

• • • ● • ● • • •

I can feel how much Yasser is struggling internally, carrying so many unspoken emotions about Talal's passing. I believe Yasser is afraid to confront the feelings he's been suppressing for so long. A heavy mix of anger and guilt weighs on his heart, keeping him trapped in his grief.

When I heard stories about Talal's final days, I felt a wave of jealousy and sadness. It hurt deeply when Farid shared how Talal had hugged him goodbye before the end. In that final embrace, Farid described every detail of Talal's face and smile. It felt as though Talal somehow knew his time was coming, and he was quietly saying his goodbyes.

I wish Yasser would allow himself to truly feel the emotions he's been buried so deeply about Talal. He needs to let those emotions surface, to move through the raw pain of grief, so he can finally begin to heal and release the burden he's been carrying.

Yasser couldn't have done anything to prevent what happened. It was Talal's time—it was out of our hands or anyone's control. Part of me longs to visit Talal's grave and speak to him there. I've been telling myself I'd go for months now. But I haven't yet mustered the courage to stand at his gravestone. I could start by standing nearby, talking to him from a distance.

Since women weren't allowed inside the cemetery, I couldn't visit his grave directly. But I kept wondering if I would finally go after returning from my trip. Part of me felt ready, yet another part hesitated. I didn't know if my grief was still about losing Talal himself or if it was tangled up in watching Yasser struggle in silence. Maybe it was both. All I knew was that the sadness felt unbearably heavy, pressing down on me in ways I still didn't fully understand.

I wish I could pour all these swirling thoughts and emotions directly into Talal. And I wish Yasser could unlock the vault he's been keeping his grief trapped inside. Letting those feelings flow freely is the only way we will ever find peace. After Talal passed away, I sent his mother a message but never received a reply. I've spoken with my cousin Nada about it. She carries such tender and beautiful stories about Talal. Nada has managed to stay in touch with Talal's mom. She reached out to her shortly after his passing, and they've kept that fragile line of connection open.

I recently asked Nada when she last spoke to Talal's mom. She said it was back in November when I sent my message. I asked Nada if Talal's mom had ever mentioned receiving my message. But Nada said no—she never brought it up. Nada promised that the next time she spoke with Talal's mom, she'd ask about my message. I hope she received it. I want so badly to connect with her, to share the weight of losing Talal—her son, my beloved friend.

I think I'm finally gathering the courage to visit Talal's grave. To stand there, speak to him, and share everything I've carried. Maybe then, this heavy ache in my heart will begin to ease.

• • • ● • ● • • •

These are some heartfelt stories I gathered from people who knew Talal. Opening up those conversations revealed so many beautiful sides of him—stories I would have never known otherwise. While some moments were overwhelmingly painful, and I had to end certain calls mid-conversation because the emotions were too raw, others brought tears to both sides. But every interaction had vulnerability, honesty, and a shared sense of healing.

I contacted Talal's siblings, my brothers—especially Yasser—and our cousins, inviting them to share whatever they felt comfortable expressing: a memory, a thought, or a feeling they missed most about him. Some spoke openly, while others chose silence—and that's okay. Grief manifests differently for everyone. Not speaking doesn't mean their love for Talal was any less; it simply means their way of processing the loss is uniquely their own.

I hope these stories bring a smile to those who loved Talal, just as they've brought smiles—and tears—to me. They might stir up forgotten memories buried deep beneath layers of sadness. But I've realized that those memories aren't lost; they're simply waiting to resurface. All it takes is the courage to face the emotions that have kept them hidden and allow ourselves to fully feel the joy and the ache of remembering.

As I listened to these stories, I uncovered layers of Talal's spirit that I hadn't fully known before. The image of him I'd carried in my mind—the angelic presence, the gentle soul—wasn't just a figment of my imagination. He truly was an angel in human form. In his short time here, he had a rare gift: the ability to be fully present with each person he encountered. In those moments, nothing else existed—no distractions, no divided attention. Just pure, undivided presence. He gave people the most precious gift: feeling deeply seen, heard, and unconditionally loved.

The stories shared here are fragments of Talal's light, which continues to shine through the hearts of those who loved him. Each memory is a thread woven into the tapestry of his legacy.

• • • • • • • • • • •

Shatha (A Special Connection)

When his story is opened for me, it never closes. I talked to my sister about him a lot; I see him in everything. The innocent part of my life. This world is too cruel for someone like Talal. As much as it hurts my heart to think about him, I am happy to talk about him for hours, and it's relieving. Until today, all major milestones in my life, I think of him. I wanted to name my second son Talal but was afraid of what relationship would be created with him. I didn't want him to be the special child.

We met at the age of 12. It was a long-distance relationship as he lives in Riyadh, and she is in Khobar, so I felt I couldn't handle it after a while. I broke off our relationship multiple times, but he always returned after a while; without context, he would reach out. I also knew that he would come back, so I felt safe. I always told him, "I know deep within me that life will bring us back together." From the bottom of my heart, I believed we would end up being married.

He was a very courageous young man. Genuine. Had good intentions all the time. He would never do something if he felt it was wrong. One time, he came to Khobar and tried to call me. I didn't answer as I wasn't ready for the relationship to start again. He called the house many, many, many times, waiting for me to pick up, but I didn't. When my family would answer the phone, he would talk to them and say hi. He never shut the phone in anyone's face. It was simply against his good manners. He sent me a message through Yasser that he would stay in front of my house until I answered, even if it meant he would sleep on the grass in my front yard. I didn't answer; he had slept on the grass all night. He truly was an angel.

The last time I ended it, he didn't reach out as usual, and a longer time passed with no communication from him, so I called that time; he had confessed to being in a relationship with someone else; her name was Nada. This person reached out to me after his death. I felt that if he valued her so much, we must share something in common. We ended up grieving together as we remembered our days with him.

On October 27th, 2004, it was a Ramadan night, and I was in Bahrain with my roommate, getting ready to leave for Sahoor with my parents. I could have a phone call from my best friend's boyfriend at the time. I was surprised to see his call and thought I wouldn't answer. He called and called and called. I didn't want to answer. My best friend called and told me to answer him as he had something urgent to tell me. I called him back, and he said Talal died in a car crash. My heart sank; I said, What? He repeated Talal died in a car crash. I shut the phone in his face and broke down crying. My roommate walked in and shouted about what was happening. I told her nothing. I dismissed the thought. I completely denied it and went out for dinner as if nothing happened. I thought to myself the call was a lie. Then I called Talal's cousin, and he said it was true. A part of me died that night. I felt my life was over; the man I loved died, and I couldn't comprehend what life would be like anymore.

The next few days were a fog. I didn't want to go to the funeral. But I pushed myself through it. When I walked in, I looked to my right side and saw a Talal guitar in a small room. I felt I wanted to explode but gathered the strength to walk into the house further. I reached the place where Dalia was sitting. She handed me some papers with prayers for Talal and a picture of him. She asked me to look at his picture; I shook my head. She insisted. I looked down and saw his face for the first time after his death. I exploded crying and sat next to Dalia with my head on her shoulder.

A few days later, I felt compassion for Nada, as if she and I had lost someone deeply important to us. We both cared for the same person, but now he was gone. I felt the need to call her as we shared a bond. It was a sad but truly amazing call, as if we were grieving and healing together.

I miss the look on his face that explains it all. I miss his kindness. He was not an open person; I had to drag from him what's going on in his head. He didn't like to bother others with his worries and concerns. I remember one summer when he returned from Germany and did not seem okay. I asked him so many times till he confessed. He was struggling with his mom having a relationship with a man. He loved her so much and was worried about her. He also loved his stepmother very much. He felt she went through a lot and suffered in her life.

Talal studied medicine because his dad wanted him to be involved in the family business. But someone like him was meant to be a doctor, a healer, and personally touch others' lives. He would have made an amazing one. It's mind-blowing how it has been almost 20 years since he passed away, but people still talk about him. People still pray for him. He touched so many lives in the short life he had.

· · · · ●·●·● · · ·

Omar (Talal's Cousin)

Talal is my cousin, and we were the same age. We both lived in Riyadh and would spend many days hanging out. He was more like a brother to me. Comprehending and processing his death was very hard for me. It shook my faith and beliefs. When I lost Talal, I felt like I lost my entire family. There was a distance between everyone. Like, Talal was the glue that held us together.

I still think of Talal often. With everything happening in the world and my life now, I could use a brother. I wrote a poem about him when he passed but was shy to share it until now.

What is Absolute Love?

Is it the feeling in a husband for his wife or in a wife for her husband?
Is it the feeling between a mother and her child, or the child for his father?
Is true friendship true love?
And if your true friendship ends, have you lost true love?
We always define love as existing between two or more people.
What about those who are alone?
If love is between people, then is love fair to those who are alone?
But isn't love absolute and divine? It must be fair.
Is our understanding that of human love and not Absolute Love?
Maybe we don't truly understand Absolute Love.
If we don't understand it, then what is it?
Some people have been gifted with the knowledge of Absolute Love.
It is those people who taught us that love is greater than what we imagine.

It is these people who told us that love is always fair to those who seek it.

It is these people who told us that love is closer to us than we ever imagined.

God is Absolute Love, Al-Wadud.

God is everywhere, they say, but most importantly, He can be found through each of us.

When God gave us His Holy Breath through Adam, He placed the ability to find absolute Love in each of our hearts.

This Holy Breath is the life force within every human, animal, and plant.

If we find God, we find absolute Love.

Then, is Love fair?

Even if you are alone, you can find Absolute Love when you find God through his Holy Breath in your own heart.

Jesus, peace and blessings be upon him, taught us to love our One God with all our hearts, all our minds, all our strength, and all our souls.

Then and only then will we meet our Lord and be one with absolute Love.

What about love between people?

Is it part of the divine gift or a distraction from the divine gift?

When one loves the God who gave him the Holy Breath, one will love the Holy Breath within others.

Love between people is a path to Absolute Love.

Muhammad, peace and blessings be upon him, taught us that we do not truly believe unless we love each other first.

"If you love your Creator, love each other first."

As both spiritual messengers taught, we will not believe in Absolute Love until we love for others as we would love for ourselves.

We do not fulfill the command to love each other first until we love all of God's creatures, everything with life.

For everything that is alive is part of God's Holy Breath.

This love is Absolute Love.

God's mercy and Love gave us life so that we may use this life to know Him.

To know Him, we must first know Absolute Love deep in our hearts.

For Him, Absolute Love is nearer to those who seek Him than their own jugular vein.

Jesus, peace and blessings be upon him, tells us that those who find Absolute Love will have eternal life.

Maybe it is through such an introduction that one may be able to fully grasp what the Prophet Muhammad, peace and blessings be upon him, meant when he said:

"Blessed is the act of planting a tree even if it is the day before the Last Day."

Although it has an important literal meaning, it has an even more potent spiritual meaning.

When we lose someone we love, it is easy to lose faith in Absolute Love.

We lose faith in the Holy Breath and the life force of Absolute Love that is God.

How can we trust the life force, which seems so fragile?

How is this Absolute Love when it gives as it pleases and takes as it pleases?

How can we believe in an Absolute Love that has not shown us love?

But that's where we are mistaken.

Absolute Love has not been taken from us, for what it took was never ours.

It has graced us with its Love with a life and then taken it back.

The life force is God's gift of Love, and that is eternal.

The agent of God's Love is mortal; that goes.

Although we may never know what this means in this life, we can never lose faith in it.

Absolute Love is a test; it can sometimes feel like a curse.

To fail the test is to leave Absolute Love.

If we leave Absolute Love, it leaves us.

Our life force dims as it loses its essence.

Maybe the greatest force to revive our faith in Absolute Love is to feel the untainted life within a plant.

The life force within it much reflects our own, as it too depends on absolute Love.

A person who plants a life force dependent on Absolute Love believes deep inside in the goodness and power of Absolute Love.

But a person who believes and trusts in Absolute Love even when life will cease everywhere around him is blessed with the gift of Absolute Love.

For this person believes that Absolute Love will triumph over all.

Maybe a spiritual interpretation would read:

"Blessed is the person who trusts and loves the life force from God even when he knows that the Love that has graced us with life will soon take it all away."

A simple plant can remind us of the Love that gave us life.

For this is the test: to not give up on Absolute Love.

Even when it seems to have left us by taking away one whom we love.

We must realize that it is there and still loves us if we love it.

A story best encapsulates this love and not giving up on Absolute Love.

The angel who took the life of someone's loved one went to God, and God asked, 'Did you take this person's loved one?'

The angel replied, "Yes."

Then God asked, "And what did this person say?"

The angel responded:

"All praise be to God, Absolute Love."

All praise be to God the All-Compassionate, All-Merciful, whose Love gave us the gift of life and who blessed the earth with His prophets and messengers so that we may be able to find Him, Absolute Love.

Amen.

Omar Breik

• • • • ● • ● • • •

Dina (Talal's Sister)

I mostly miss his company, calmness, hugs, and shy smile (his "you got me" smile).

Memories of him visiting and spending time with my kids Muneeb and Judy.

Most profound was his last visit. His childhood and clinginess when he first came to Saudi.

• • • ● • ● • • •

Mahmoud (Dina's Husband)

I have simple yet very sentimental memories of Talal. I remember when he went to university in Khobar and would visit our home frequently. He enjoyed my mother's cooking and was fond of cabbage rolls (Malfoof), which my mother still remembers.

He was an amazing uncle to Muneeb and Judy. He played with them and held them with so much love, reminding me of my relationships with my nieces and nephews. He often made me wish I could have seen him grow to be a big part of not only Muneeb and Judy's lives but also Joanne and Khalid's.

I admired his comfortability with me and Dina's relationship as newlyweds, making me feel welcomed into the family even more than I already was, trusting me and respecting me, even when asked by his father to keep an eye on us; I found that funny.

He was a ray of sunshine and a joy to be around. I saw him as a son and wish I could have seen him grow up to be the successful man he had so much potential.

· · · ● ● ● ● ● · ·

Farid (Talal's College Roommate)

I remember him always, but a crystal-clear memory of him was the last time I saw him in Ramadan at around 3 p.m. He knocked on my door and said, "Farid, I'm going to Riyadh now. Yasser had a car accident, but he is okay, so I'm going to drive there." He said goodbye, hugged, and smiled at me. I told him goodbye and good luck on your fencing tournament. That hug, smile, and every detail of him were very different and sincere. He always cared for, asked about, and updated us.

He was the calmest person I have ever met. For example, he could be very good at studying, but he also managed to live fully, have hobbies, and make time for himself and others. He was always present for us; he would give us his full attention when he sat with us. He would truly listen, talk, and give advice. He was attached to his guitar and, very sensible and romantic, listened to soft music; he was very different from us teenage boys. He had a gentle touch.

I remember the last summer he returned from Germany; he told me he worked in an elderly home. He spent time with senior people and saw a lot of deaths. He lived with people who didn't make it. Since that time, he has been different. Talking about being better, doing good to people, being close to

God, and staying away from sins. He was determined to be a better person. Three months later, he died. I think he felt that his time to leave this world was coming. He gave everyone his time.

I miss the times we always joked with him. He would get angry fast, and he had a short temper, but in a funny way. He was an amazing friend. I could tell him any secret, and I told him a lot of secrets. He would never judge and always kept my secrets, which only shows me that he had a big heart and was raised well.

• • • • • • • • •

Osama (My Father)

The first time I met Talal. It was in Paris, and I saw a cute 7-month-old blond baby boy. His parents were so happy to have him. At that time, he was not yet introduced to the rest of the family. The next time I saw him was in Riyadh; he could only speak English then. His father had to go to work, and Talal was crying so much that his father called Yasmine (Dalia's mother) to bring Dalia and Yasser to entertain him. I can't forget him as he ran around the house repeating, "I want my daddy; I want my daddy." He was not used to the people in the house yet. I remember him wearing tight white pajamas with drawings on them. He was so innocent and scared because he was attached to his father. It broke my heart how sad he was. I tried to calm him down, saying, "Your daddy is coming back soon." Dalia and Yasser were sitting and watching, not knowing what was happening.

I also remember the first day after Ramadan (Eid) when we got Talal and Yasser a black plane toy. He was so happy, playing with it, excited and joyful.

But what I remember the most is how happy his father was as he watched his son be so happy. His father truly loved him so much. I can't forget how Talal always wrote letters to his dad, and it made his father proud. I remember he used to brag about these letters to us.

We keep talking about Talal's relationship with his father, but let's not forget that there is a mother out there who is most probably devastated that her son is not living with her. I remember sensing a rivalry in the household about Talal being so spoiled. I guess it's normal for this to happen in a house of many children of different mothers.

I remember when he came to visit me in the USA at 15, along with Yasser. That was the time I found out that he had a spiritual side to him, and I was happy for him. He told me that he was caught talking to a girl one day by his stepmother (whom he loves and respects a lot). She talked with him and asked him, "Would you like it if boys talked to your sisters?" He said no and promised to stop and leave all this materialistic world for God and the love of God. His love of God and principles was embedded in him because of his stepmother (Oma Ursula). I believe this will be in their good deeds.

After getting divorced from Dalia's mother, I asked Yasser about Talal and how he is doing, as I stopped seeing him after the divorce. I told Yasser to ask Talal to keep bringing his clothes for laundry to our house as he always did the year he moved to Khobar. Yasser told Talal this, and he replied, "Yasser, I miss your father and would love to see him." I remember Yasser often going to Talal and sleeping in his house.

I remember Talal's soft looks and the details of his soft face. Only once was he so angry that he talked to me for advice. I tried to calm him down, as I had never seen him this angry because he had found out his sister was talking to a boy.

I remember when he came to me in Dubai with Yasser, and they ate all the chocolate from the mini bar in the hotel room. I remember it so clearly because the bill was so high for people at work; they thought i drank alcohol, and im a religious man.

I will not forget the day when my uncle Mazin (who was Talal's father's heart doctor) was called to tell him that his son had died. He went to his house at night as he was sitting there waiting for his son to come home. When he saw his cardiologist instead, he looked at him and said, "What are you doing here?" with anger and fear in his voice, as if deep down inside he knew. When the news was broken to him, he said to my uncle, "Parents are not meant to bury their children."

The next day, after prayer on Talal in the mosque, we went to the graveyard, and they brought his body down from the car to place him in his grave; the doctor carrying him was shouting out, "MAY GOD BE WITH YOU, DR. WAEL (TALAL'S FATHER), MAY GOD GIVE YOU PATIENCE!" over and over again. I was crying. Everyone was crying. Those who knew him and who didn't know him were crying. I don't remember seeing my sons because I was crying so much. I went over to his father and kissed him many, many, many times.

Talal was brave and loved God. His life was too short. People usually remember their parents or grandparents if they have seen them long enough or if they have seen someone who impacted their lives. Tala impacted people close to him, like his father, mother, youngest sister Sarah, and Yasser. I did not know that Dalia was still grieving him. Finally, I think Talal is in a better place today.

• • • ● • ● • • •

Rayyan (Dalia's Brother)

Although I was young when he passed (10 years old), I have loads of moments with him, but one that sticks out. We were playing a soccer game on PlayStation, and although I was young, I was much better than him at the game. I remember he had just come from Riyadh by car and was tired but wanted to play with me. I was winning, but I felt for him because he was tired, and I let him win the game to make him feel better. He was celebrating scoring goals, and I was just happy that he was happy. Favorite memory of him, no doubt. Glad I gave him that moment.

• • • ● • ● • • •

Nour (Talal's Niece)

I use his passing as a landmark in my calendar for many things that happened during the same time. A few big memories that stuck with me from him were when he would visit us for dinner once a week to get his laundry done at our home. He would also help me with my French homework as he spoke (English, Arabic, French, and German). I remember asking him why I had to learn this "stupid language"; he said something so moving I still have it in mind to this day. He said the Prophet Mohammad told his people it is always best to understand the language of others. I suddenly took it as a mission to learn it better.

Another memory was when I asked him to teach me to play the guitar, as I remember he had one that he brought over a few times.

He had a beautiful soul, and now, looking back at those memories, it's hard to believe how young he was for such a mature person.

· · · · ● · ● · · ·

Musbah (May's Husband)

I never fully comprehended the intense emotions his death caused me personally. I truly miss his serenity. May God bless all our departed.

· · · · ● · ● · · ·

Sami (Talal's Nephew)

Although my memories of Talal are weak, I remember the severity of the loss within the family, even at a young age. And can see the large void it has left in the family. On a positive note, remember that he was very family-oriented and engaged. This makes me think often, even today, how different my life, Dalia's, my grandfather's, and all our lives would be if he were still here. That is always a happy imagination.

· · · · ● · ● · · ·

Ali (Talal's Nephew)

I think of him a lot. It was hard growing older without his influence as a role model. I always find it amazing what an impact he had at such a young age. I am grateful that all my memories of him are good ones.

· · ● · ● · ● ● · ·

Yasmine (Talal's Eldest Sister and My Mom)

I miss him and feel cheated out of a younger brother and a soulmate in terms of both of us being taken from our mothers. I always had that connection with him because my father has done to him exactly what he has done to me. For a while, I struggled to understand why God would take a young boy so soon. But my main sadness was for my children, who must go through this and grief at a young age.

I miss his smile, even his temper, and all his history that we never got to share because he died: career, marriage, kids. Generally, I barely knew him as a sibling because I was already married and out of the house when he was born and came to Saudi. My memories are mostly in my grandparents' house. However, my memories of Talal are mostly related to my children, who grew up together.

· · ● · ● · ● ● · ·

Gabrielle (Talal's Mother)

I have texted her with no reply. I can't start to imagine the pain she is going through. The anger towards my grandfather for taking her son from her. Deep down inside me, I know he didn't do it with bad intentions. Wrong was his doing, but he meant well. As an old-fashioned, traditional, conservative Muslim man, he was probably thinking of keeping all his children under one roof and raising them to be good Muslim people.

My grandmother Christa, who suffered the same as Talal's mother, kept two pages from a German magazine named Bunte for all these years, which was issued on 29 May 1991. The article's title was "I protest in front of the embassy, I write letters, and I distribute flyers. I will continue on my path until the end." Below are excerpts from this article.

> *Gabriele Ittenbach, 39, foreign language secretary, delicate and pale, sits in her 35 sqm apartment in Paris, 6th floor, and talks about the abduction of her son. Kidnapping by the father, a Saudi millionaire, 54. She no longer speaks his name. She only refers to him as "the father of my son." She loved him. But he amputated a part of her body like a surgeon without anesthesia—the child.*
>
> *It is the perverse repetition of the successful thriller "Not Without My Daughter" by American author Betty Mahmoody. Only now, the victim is a German, and the child is a son. Mrs. Ittenbach looks at the yellow daisies in a crystal vase over her bed on the full bookshelf and says, "I spoke to Mrs. Mahmoody. She said I must not give up. I must fight." The fight has cost her 30,000 marks and has changed her.*
>
> *It was two years ago. A humid Sunday. She had been in the countryside. Her ex-husband came up the stairs in a Parisian tailored suit, not in a kaftan; he laughed as always. He told the nanny, I'll take the son with me for a short while. He wrote a little note: "Dear Gabriele, I have taken Talal on a trip for a few days to satisfy his desire for vacation so he doesn't*

feel alone and abandoned again. We will get in touch. Maybe you want to come along too. Otherwise, don't worry and have a good time."

Gabriele Ittenbach never saw her son again. She wrote letters, unsure if her son ever received them—Riyadh, Saudi Arabia, care of post office. She protests in front of the Saudi embassy in Paris. She goes to the police. She waits in front of the house in Hamburg that still belongs to her ex-husband. She goes to Amnesty International and distributes flyers. Her ex-husband is convicted—one year of imprisonment and a 50,000 franc fine. A verdict that doesn't apply in the desert. Her son has disappeared.

Memories. The man. She says, "I met him while having dinner here in Paris. He spoke German and studied medicine in Hamburg. He was so charming, very charming. I fell in love with him, even though he had already been married to two German women. Both had children with him. I became his lover and saw myself as his third wife. He was full of life, drank wine and whiskey, and took me to Maxim's. After a year, he said, 'I want a son from you!' When you're in love, you're blind and trusting. But the father of my son changed. He suddenly brought a prayer rug. He knelt three times a day, facing Mecca. He became a macho. He commanded me. I had been his birthing slave. He became a Sunday daddy and came once a month. Always brought gifts, teddy bears, and airplane models. My son loved him."

The memory hurts. Gabriele Ittenbach wants to go for a walk to a café. We have a glass of champagne. Her hand still trembles. Her voice became louder and faster, and her throat turned red: "At that time, I hardly ate or slept. I just cried. Lost ten kilograms. After that, I only felt hatred for the father of my son. If I had found him, maybe I would have killed him. But I wouldn't have been able to leave the city anymore; I know that. Acquaintances held me back. I would have been lost."

She last heard her son's voice a year ago, on Julian's 23rd birthday. The French ambassador arranged a phone call: "Hello, darling!" - "Hello, Mommy!" - "How are you?" - Silence - "Are you doing well?" - "Yes." Her son only says yes or no. The mother: "My son is torn apart, completely silent. This silence is worse than crying. I feel that he no longer resists. I feel his longing for me, and I know he lives alone in a villa with air conditioning."

She lowers her Madonna-like face: "Fate is like a knife. If you hold it the wrong way, you cut yourself. The terrible thing is that it takes so long to learn how to handle it. Maybe I touched it wrong too many times. I must fight. I am a mother fighting for her child. I won't give up." She cries."

26 BUNTE. From the article "BUNTE." Issue 23 of 295.1991

The article talks about an interview with Talal's mother as she was looking for her little boy. I translated it, and a mix of emotions hit me hard. Between the fact that she was in so much pain at the time and for her, the pain had surely grown when he died. But I also felt sad that the picture made it seem like Talal was an unhappy child. It truly hurts my heart.

I remember traveling on holidays with my mother, father, and Yasser. We met Talal, my grandfather, and Talal's mother in Syria and Egypt. I was very young, but I remember swimming in hotel pools with them with lots of joy and laughter. As a child, that's what my brain could comprehend. I didn't realize there was pain behind it all.

I often wonder that maybe Talal has not comprehended his trauma as a young boy, but had he become an adult, would he have dealt with it? I don't know.

• • • ● • ● • • •

When Grief Seems to Be Every Where
The Inescapable Presence of Loss

Though sincere tributes filled the air at the funeral, a great gloom hung like a dense cloud. Every member of my family, friends, and even I carried grief in different ways.

Years later, yet shadows of quiet loomed over us. We never spoke about Talal—about how we felt when he died or the weight of life without him. I was the only one who dared to break the silence, gently asking my family to share their grief, but the silence remained.

Despite the passing years, talking about Talal felt like trying to touch something fragile and sacred—something no one dared to break.

• • • •●• •●• • •

I'm unsure where I found the courage to speak up when others couldn't finally. In February 2023, a major change gave me that bravery. After 17 years of dedication as a nurse in Khobar, I decided to leave my job.

I was offered the role of Director of Nursing—a dream I had worked towards for years. But life had other plans when my family's move to Riyadh became inevitable.

The decision was incredibly tough—I had worked hard for that role. But with my husband's transfer to Riyadh and our children starting new schools, the path forward was clear.

Choosing my family over a long-cherished career goal gave me unexpected strength. That choice made me brave enough to finally break the silence about Talal after years of holding it all inside.

I only had two days to decide whether to accept the director position. It felt like an impossible choice. But in the end, I turned it down to move to Riyadh with my husband and kids.

At first, having no work and nothing to do felt incredibly strange after years of constant busyness. I tried picking up hobbies I'd always wanted to start—crocheting, painting, yoga—but each attempt faded after a few weeks.

That sabbatical year became a bridge between the life I had built in Khobar and the one waiting for me in Riyadh. Though it was strange and disturbing, it also allowed me to breathe—that is, stop and realize who I was, free from the weight of my job and habit tying me down.

· · · ● · ● · ● · ·

Being alone at home proved more difficult than I had anticipated. I was empty, as though something essential was absent. I stuffed my days with constant distractions to escape facing those emotions. I watched TV shows nonstop, *Grey's Anatomy* episode after episode, desperate to keep my head busy and quiet during those silent times.

But finally, the distractions ceased to be effective. Alone with my ideas, I became aware that dark and depressing thoughts dominated my mind. That quiet offered no escape from them.

That year off let me come to some tough conclusions. My work behind me and my children in school left me wondering who I was. I had always defined myself as a nurse, and the director position had become my identity. But without those titles, I asked myself, *"Who am I?"*

That search for identity led me inward—to better understand myself. The first step was letting out the emotions I had bottled up for far too long.

I started gently removing the layers and allowed myself to feel instead of fleeing. Every cry and every heavy breath drew me toward the version of me I had long buried under years of obligation and preoccupation.

· · · ● ● ● ● ● · ·

When we moved to Riyadh, I noticed something. Whenever I met someone new, I immediately told them about Talal. It was as if I needed everyone to know this integral part of my story to validate his importance in my life. Back in Khobar, I didn't need to explain about Talal. Everyone already knew him, witnessed his death, and shared in the grief, whether silently or openly. My life with Talal was understood.

But in this new city, no one knew that side of me. So, I constantly mentioned Talal to prove to others that he was real and meaningful. And every time I spoke about him, I suddenly cried, even with people I barely knew. It felt like the grief was still raw, lingering under the surface, waiting for an opportunity to spill out.

That's when I realized there was a part of my healing process I hadn't gone through yet. I needed to fully process what happened with Talal. I had to go back to that day he died and grieve it all over again from the start. I had to let those feelings and memories pour out of me completely.

I thus started letting myself go back to experience those events and let my feelings run free. I cried about Talal, spoke about Talal, and kept remembering Talal till it stopped feeling so weighty. Every tear and discussion made me feel lighter, as though I had let another bit of the loss I had stashed free.

This was the grieving process I needed but hadn't given myself permission for until now. I let all the feelings out, let them flow through me, not holding anything back.

I couldn't move forward until I fully accepted what happened by feeling it again from the very beginning.

Little by little, by being open and vulnerable about my loss, I started to find some peace. The grief didn't disappear, but I could breathe easier, carrying less of that weight alone inside me. I finally grieved Talal's death in the way I needed to heal.

· • • ● • ● • • ·

For many years, I was a real workaholic. I worked tirelessly as a nurse, throwing myself into every task, every shift. Looking back, I realize now that this was my way of escaping from grief. Work became my shelter—a place where I could stay so busy that I wouldn't have to confront the heavy sadness I carried deep inside.

It wasn't just Talal's death; I was grieving. I carried other griefs, too, like the day my daughter was diagnosed with type-1 diabetes. Finding out she had this illness felt like losing the healthy child I had envisioned. It was a different kind of loss, but it was grief all the same.

This gloom struck me more strongly than ever during the COVID-19 epidemic in 2020. Instead of sitting with those emotions, though, I buried myself even more in my work. My days became a haze of administrative chores, hospital rounds, and ongoing obligations.

Work was my escape route, my way of running from the overwhelming emotions tied to Talal's loss and my daughter's illness. As long as I kept moving and working, I didn't have to stop and face what awaited me in the silence.

If I didn't slow down, I didn't have to confront those difficult, big griefs weighing me down.

Around this time, Yasser made a big change in his life. He had been studying at a university in Saudi Arabia, but shortly after Talal's passing, he decided to continue his studies in the United States.

I've often wondered whether this move was an escape or a fresh start. My family never openly discussed it. Grief had turned into silence between us, and Yasser carried his emotions quietly, in his own way.

While he was away at school, he sent emails to my parents and uncle. In those messages, he expressed guilt over Talal's death—guilt that he somehow felt responsible for something he had no control over.

Perhaps going to the States was Yasser's way of escaping that guilty pain he felt.

We never talked about it. Silence, once again, stood between us. I've often questioned whether Yasser's decision was a conscious escape or simply the next step in his life. Maybe it was neither.

Grief does unusual things to people. Some flee, others immerse themselves in distractions, while yet others shut down totally. Perhaps Yasser was seeking to establish a new normal—a life removed from the weight of shared trauma—by moving to the United States.

Ultimately, Yasser and I discovered our coping mechanisms: his from distance, mine from constant labor. Underneath it all, though, we both silently, alone, held our pain until we felt ready to confront it.

· · · · ● · ● · · ·

In those first painful days after Talal's passing, my mother tried offering some comfort. She would say spiritual things like *"After hardship, goodness will come"* and *"Be patient; better times lie ahead."* But her reassuring words were very brief. She didn't have the strength to offer me much more than that.

Only a year after Talal died, I married my husband, Sami. He had known me when the tragedy occurred, but we weren't engaged then. Sami never got to meet Talal himself.

Before our marriage, there wasn't much support for me in grieving Talal's loss. But after we wed, Sami witnessed how heavily I carried that grief. He saw me breaking down in tears constantly over little reminders. A sad song would play in the car, and I'd suddenly sob.

During those moments, Sami's response was a gift. He never said unhelpful phrases like, *"What's wrong?"* or *"Don't cry, it's okay."* Instead, he would gently say, *"Deal with it. Cry and process it—I'm here for you."*

Sami's supportive presence in that first year gave me a safe space to grieve freely and without judgment. He allowed me to cry, feel, and fully accept my sadness without interference.

However, when the second year of grieving came around, I started questioning how much longer I could keep this up. I thought to myself, *"This is ridiculous. How many more years will I cry for?"*

Even though I wasn't fully done grieving yet, I chose to start suppressing those emotions. I realized I had cried every single day during that first year of grief. But eventually, I felt the need to carry my grief differently.

I forced myself to stop crying and cut off thoughts about the loss. Whenever a song or something reminded me of Talal, I blocked it out completely. For four years, I avoided my grandfather's home in Riyadh, where the funeral was held. I even avoided driving down the highway where Talal's accident occurred.

Around six years after his death, I stumbled upon a picture of Talal. Seeing his face after so long brought a wave of emotions—sadness, happiness, warmth, and familiarity.

There were two separate chapters to my grieving process. The first was bursting with uncontrollably frequent anguish and tears. After that, though, I started totally suppressing those feelings. I pushed my grief aside and stopped dealing with it rather than keeping it under reasonable control.

This repression persisted for over two decades—18 or 19 years—until I decided deliberately to face my loss squarely. I came to see I had to go back over those feelings, really feel them, and let myself heal correctly.

In those early grief stages, there was no hopefulness, no light. Only the heavy weight of loss, hopelessness, and helplessness. I fantasized about things returning to normal, about a world where Talal wasn't gone. Those were very, very dark times.

But over the past couple of years, I've worked hard to change my relationship with grief. I've learned to create space to process it healthily instead of suppressing it entirely or drowning in it hopelessly.

Little by little, I'm making peace with carrying Talal's memory forward while still feeling joy in the present moment.

When Talal died, it felt like the entire world had crashed down around me. My sadness was so deep, so consuming, that it was hard to keep going each day. Even my mother's kind words— *"After hardship, goodness will come"* and *"Be patient; better times lie ahead"*—couldn't pull me out of that dark place.

When I got married, Sami became my rock. He comforted me when sadness over losing Talal washed over me again and again. He held me as I cried and gave me the space to feel my emotions fully.

Even with Sami's encouragement, though, I was reluctant to confront my loss squarely. I worried about the rawness of my grief and the finality of embracing Talal—totally gone forever.

Every time Talal came up, I pushed them away. Anything that would force me to face the truth of his loss was avoided. Still, I felt not at ease, even with all that avoidance.

Eventually, I decided to face my suffering head-on instead of retreating from it. I began letting myself really feel Talal's loss and grieve him with my full heart.

I let his smile, laugh, and hugs flow over me. I went over every element of our time together, the way things were before he left. I felt the hurt once more, but instead of trying to ignore it this time, I leaned into it.

It turned into a spiritual trip—a way for me to embrace rather than run from my loss. Carrying the weight of Talal's loss without holding back, I showed up totally for the sadness.

My connection with God gave me the strength for this journey. It allowed me to surrender to my experience instead of trying to control or contain it.

So much good came from this spiritual opening—an opening to confront my real experience of missing Talal.

Through this confrontation came a new sense of freedom. I realized that grief doesn't disappear, but it transforms. My relationship with it changed as I created space for all my difficult feelings, allowing them to flow instead of suppressing them.

From this transparency came an overpowering sense of love—not romantic love but an unqualified love that filled me up. It encircled me like a nice, consoling hug.

My perspective of the world started to be built on this love. Difficulties were greeted with compassion and kindness instead of triggering wrath or dread.

One really difficult incident I recall occurred at work with a colleague who had recently lost her mother. She projected her suffering onto me and attacked me angrily and frustratingly.

I might have closed down or rebelled in the past. But I matched her fury with love at that same instant. After she finished, I let her vent, gave her room, and softly rested my palm on hers.

She started to cry; her shields collapsed. It was a healing time for me as much as for her.

Love turned into my unquestionable base and source of strength and peace.

Along this road, I have come to see that loss is not something one can conquer or wipe out. One carries with love, acceptance, and thankfulness something like this.

The love I still carry for Talal includes every tear, memory, and anguish. Today, I carry it as a holy component of who I am, not weighed down by it.

• • • ● • ● • • •

Visiting Talal's Grave

I planned to visit Talal's grave for the first time during the last ten days of Ramadan 2024. The morning of our visit, I woke up feeling incredibly peaceful. It's the holiest time of the month, and somehow, it just felt right in my heart. My intuition told me this was the moment.

At first, we had planned to visit on Sunday, but my husband had work commitments, and the plan fell through. Eventually, we decided on Tuesday—it worked for everyone, and I wanted my husband to be there. Of course, I also chose my husband and best friend, who had mentored me through this spiritual journey of becoming more conscious and aware.

Fear crept in as the day started. Part of me wanted to back off from facing the feelings I knew would come up. Stopped, I asked myself, *"Why am I scared?"* The answer came: I was afraid of how I might react or break down.

"What's the worst that could happen? I might cry. And that's okay," I whispered silently.

I felt like I had reached a point in my grief where I could talk about Talal, remember him, and think about him without tears. But a part of me worried that visiting his grave would unravel all that.

A quieter voice inside me said, *"No more crying; you're done with that."* But another voice said, *"No, it's okay to feel. It's okay to cry."*

The fear started to fade, replaced by a strange sense of calm. I took slow, deep breaths and imagined myself sitting quietly at his graveside. If tears streamed down my cheeks while memories of my dear Talal washed over me, those tears would be a sacred expression of love.

Crying at Talal's gravesite wouldn't be the end of the world. My heart was open to whatever needed to be felt or released.

An unusual sense of calm washed over me. I felt serene, and my heart felt wide open, ready to embrace the day ahead and everyone around me.

• • • ● • ● • • •

When we planned to leave home at 5 o'clock, we packed supplies for our trip to the desert after the graveyard visit. We gathered food, firewood, and anything else we might need, then got in the car and hit the road.

The graveyard was an hour's drive from our home. Since I was still new to Riyadh, the streets looked completely unfamiliar, especially the southern areas. I had no idea where we were during most of the drive.

But I experienced a change as we neared the cemetery. Heavy and relentless, a tsunami of anguish and sadness slammed on my chest.

Tears welled up as a clear picture of a car exactly like ours drove Talal's dead body down this same road across my thoughts. I felt as if I was there, accompanying him on his final journey.

"I'm okay, I'm okay," I whispered under my breath, trying to calm the storm inside me. But my heart raced, and my chest tightened with grief and fear.

Though I tried so hard to get ready, the rawness of loss crept back in.

I froze when we finally reached the cemetery gates. Before us lay a large walled space emanating nearly holy silence.

"Is that it?" I asked quietly. Driving, my pal nodded gravely and said, *"Yes, this is it."*

The air seemed weighty but also quite calm. Sensing its great presence, I gazed at the tomb. Though I hadn't been there for Talal's funeral, my heart seemed oddly linked to this hallowed site.

· · · ● · ● ● · · ·

I observed a part on the left side of the graveyard that seemed to be softly guiding me as we rounded the borders of the cemetery.

My husband asked, *"Do you want to go down?"* after stopping the automobile once more.

I hesitated. *"I don't think I'm allowed to."*

But he replied softly, *"Never mind the rules right now. What do you want to do?"*

Looking around at the quiet graveyard, I whispered, *"I want both of you to get out and leave me alone for a bit."*

They stepped out of the car without a word, leaving me alone in the stillness.

As their footsteps faded away, the floodgates opened. Sobs trembled through me wave after wave. I permitted every drop, every raw feeling, to run wild; I did not try to stop them.

"Hi, Talal. I'm here. I miss you so much, more and more every day that passes. I really, really love you."

I closed my eyes and let myself fully feel every ounce of grief, love, and longing.

"I'm okay now. I know you're okay, too. I'm just telling you I'm alright. Thank you for always being with me."

Although I sat beside the place holding Talal's physical remains, I knew his spirit was not confined to this grave.

"When I leave, I'll say goodbye to your body. But I know your spirit and soul are with me constantly. You live within me always."

For about fifteen tranquil minutes, I sat still, enveloped in the quiet power of that sacred space. My mind stopped racing, and I *was* fully present in the moment.

When I was ready, I signaled my husband by knocking on the car window. The same holy silence around us all softened his face as he and my friend came back. *"Are you ready to go now? Or do you need more time?"*

"No, I'm good," I replied with a lightness I hadn't felt in years.

As we drove away, I turned back to look at the graveyard. The sun was setting, casting long shadows across the weathered stones.

"Goodbye, Talal. Until we meet again."

A sense of peace lingered in my chest, warm and steady.

Letting Go of Deep Grief
Releasing the Weight While Holding the Love

I lost clarity when Talal passed away. The loss felt disorganized, with memories and emotions pouring in without any direction or structure.

I recalled talks about pausing from work to sort out who I really was outside of titles or duties at that time. I was looking for simple clarity about my real self, not for deep explanations.

I started attending wellness resorts emphasizing yoga, meditation, and inner healing. These places let me discover a world I had not before ventured into. One especially noteworthy event in Riyadh was a gathering full of people using various types of mindfulness and self-expression.

This event featured an *"ecstatic dance."* Though two friends were anxious to join and pushed me to go along, I had never heard of it before. Originally, I hesitated. Dancing in front of people was scary, and I have always been rather judgmental of myself. I chose, nonetheless, to venture beyond my comfort zone.

Every dance, the teacher said, stood for one of the four natural elements: water, fire, air, and earth. Every component carried movement, energy, and rhythm. The music included strong drumbeats for fire, and we were instructed to stomp our feet hard into the ground to replicate cracking flames.

Between each dance segment, we were told to close our eyes, take deep breaths, and center ourselves. When we opened our eyes, we had to make eye contact with someone in the room—the first person our gaze landed on. We would then sit across from them and silently gaze into their eyes without speaking.

The first time, I ended up across from a young man in his twenties. It made one uncomfortable and unpleasant. Both of us fidgeted and avoided making too lengthy eye contact. I tried to reassure him softly, *"It's okay. Just relax. You're fine."* After what felt like an eternity, but was probably less than a minute, the instructor guided us back into the next dance.

In the second round, I deliberately sought out a woman, thinking it would feel less uncomfortable. Surprisingly, it felt just as awkward, and I realized the discomfort wasn't about the other person—it was about me and the vulnerability of being seen so deeply.

By the third round, my eyes caught one of my close pals. Something changed when we fixed each other in the eyes. The discomfort subsided, and an unspoken bond surfaced. In that common silence, I felt understood in a manner words could never do.

Among the stomping feet and booming music, for a split second, I sensed a fracture in the walls I had erected around my grief. It was a little opening, a taste of what it felt like to let myself be completely present, raw, and seen—not a big breakthrough.

Though apparently basic, this encounter seeds something. Healing is not necessarily about big actions or radical insights. Sometimes, it's in the quiet of a shared look, the vulnerability of being seen, and the bravery to show up despite the discomfort.

And for that moment, amidst the dance and the silence, I felt a flicker of peace in the storm of my grief.

· · · · ● · ● · · ·

I knew we would have to do the eye-gazing again after each dance, so I decided to try finding a girl for the next round instead. *"Let me see what that experience is like,"* I thought.

My eyes caught a girl's, and we sat facing each other to gaze. I felt extremely uncomfortable this time. The young man seemed more uncomfortable than me earlier, but now, I feel exposed and uneasy with the girl.

She peered closely into my eyes, as if she were gazing right toward my soul. *"Oh My God, what is she doing?"* I considered this. I wasn't ready to show someone that sensitive side of me. I stood up fast as soon as the lesson finished, nearly running away.

"Okay," I told myself, *"I'll choose someone I already know next time. Whoever my eyes land on first from my friend group—that'll feel safer."*

When the time came again, my gaze landed on one of my friends. We sat across from each other, and I told myself, *"Allow him to look into your soul."*

Something incredible happened. As we gazed into each other's eyes, my breathing became fast and heavy. It felt like I was having an out-of-body experience, as if observing us from above.

In that intense stillness, it felt like we were having a silent conversation—an unspoken exchange of thoughts and feelings. I asked silently, *"What is this feeling?"* And in my mind, I felt answers coming back to me.

I couldn't tell if my friend was also having this experience, as we never discussed it afterward. But it was one of the most profound and unexplainable moments I had ever experienced.

I excitedly shared the story with my husband and kids. I felt almost euphoric, as if my heart had been wide open. That feeling of inner peace and love stayed with me for days afterward.

Everything felt lighter. The air, the moments, and even how I interacted with people seemed infused with this unexplainable serenity. Though I knew it had changed something deep inside me, I did not quite know what had transpired during that amazing encounter.

The vitality of that encounter stayed with me, and I found myself pulled to better grasp it. That's when my hunt for solutions started, and I stumbled down an unanticipated spiritual road.

• • • ● • ● • • •

My heart overflowed with love that I could spread to everyone around me. Everything looked brighter and more beautiful. I had no worries about the future and no regrets from the past. I existed fully in the present moment, completely conscious of the here and now.

Do you know what they call the *power of being present in the now?* I had tapped into a true consciousness of the present moment, so I didn't dwell on the past or stress about the future. I could enjoy and appreciate the amazing *now* I was experiencing.

Though at the moment, I couldn't grasp this significant change I had experienced. Everything gets analyzed and made meaningful in my brain.

I thus became motivated to find out what had happened to me on that breathtaking trip with my friend.

I began reading books and looking up responses online. Curious as well, my friend sent me that significant change. We started together reading lessons from spiritual leaders and intellectuals. We came onto the wisdom and deep lessons on *Living in The Now* of Ram Dass. For my friend, Ram Dass turned into a lighthouse of direction. Another friend joined us, having also had a transforming eye-gazing experience with someone else. The three of us started getting together regularly, creating our own circle to discuss ideas and investigate this unusual and lovely sensation.

Slowly, we realized we were walking down a spiritual path. Conversations about *the power of now* and *letting go of fear* resonated deeply with sacred verses from the *Quran*. Teachings we had grown up with started to make new sense. But we also realized that this experience wasn't confined to religion—it was tapping into something universal. We had discovered a shared spiritual language, transcending labels and boundaries. A deeper truth connected us all—a truth rooted in love, peace, and the sacredness of the present moment.

Whenever I slipped out of that blissful, peaceful state of mind, I felt an intense longing to return to that spiritual zone. Once you experience such profound inner peace and conscious presence, you crave it. You can't forget it, nor can you ignore its call. In that spiritual awakening, love isn't something you chase or seek—it becomes who you are. You embody and radiate love, not as an emotion but as an unshakable state of being.

• • • • **•** • **•** • • •

It was only later, after coming back into my body and mind, that I started feeling emotions again about the message—that death isn't painful; it just *"feels like death."* I thought, *"Oh, so Talal didn't suffer when he died. I'm relieved to receive that reassurance."*

This whole spiritual path made me realize that I must strive for constant inner peace and connection with the Divine, whatever name I give to that higher power.

The journey within myself had to start first before I could align with the sacred energy flowing upwards towards God.

That's why teachings about *chakras*, or the energy centers within our bodies, became so important to me.

Our spiritual energy flows unobstructed toward the Divine realm when all our chakras are balanced and aligned. However, that energy flow becomes blocked if our chakras are out of balance.

My inner work started then with knowing what each *chakra* stands for and how to maintain their balance and openness. To bring my *chakras* into line, I began working on particular motions, meditations, and breathwork exercises.

These practices helped me reach that *Zen* state for a while. But as soon as the busyness of regular life returned, I fell out of alignment again.

My question was, "How *can I constantly integrate this peace and stay in that enlightened state?"*

The more I read spiritual teachings, asked questions, talked to others on the path, and studied the *Quran* and sacred texts, the more I realized that they all emphasized the same core lesson: *"Know thyself."*

The spiritual teachings showed me that to know myself and find lasting inner peace truly, I had to unlock and release all the traumas, negative feelings, and *"demons"* I had buried deep inside.

The anger, hatred, envy, jealousy—all those toxic emotions—had been suppressed for so long.

They needed to come pouring out. I couldn't just read about spiritual concepts. I had to endure the hard work of dealing with all those trapped energies and unhealed wounds.

And truthfully, I'm still not done with that process even now. The inner work of confronting traumas is an ongoing journey without a final destination.

But I've come to accept that this journey isn't about reaching some ultimate state of perfection. It's about continuously showing up for myself, peeling back the layers, and allowing love and light to flow freely.

This spiritual alignment isn't a destination; it's a practice, a way of being—one breath, one moment, one conscious step at a time.

· · · · ● · ● · · ·

I once experienced a really unsettling event on a family vacation when I was just five years old.

I wandered off by myself somehow and found myself taking an elevator by myself. I have no idea where I thought I was going at the time—maybe I thought I was going to our hotel room.

But I soon realized I wasn't alone in that elevator. A man, one of the hotel staff workers, was in there with me. As a tiny 5-year-old girl looking up at this tall stranger, I immediately sensed darkness and something deeply unsettling about him.

His eyes were cold, emotionless, and distant as he stared down at me. Then, terrifyingly, he crouched down to my level and pulled at the bottom of my swimsuit. He looked at me like no adult should ever look at a child.

Having broken me like that, he turned back into my innocent five-year-old eyes and grinned. Still, I still see that terrible smile frozen in time.

I bolted out, frantically attempting to make my way back to my parents as the elevator doors opened. Where I was or what had just transpired eluded me.

I remember knocking on a random hotel room door. A kind woman opened it—an Asian woman, if my memory serves me right. After that moment, everything became blurry.

For years, I believed I had dealt with and processed that traumatic incident from my childhood. At 18, I finally spoke to my parents about it, bringing the memory to light. Therapy brought it back up again, and my therapist had me visualize my 5-year-old self sitting in front of me.

I spoke to that little girl version of myself, whispering words of comfort: *"It's okay, you're safe now."*

But recently, I realized there were still unhealed layers of that trauma deeply embedded in my body and soul.

I had to delay an appointment one day because I needed an emergency breathing session with a trauma-release specialist visiting from Turkey. His breathwork techniques are designed to help people unlock and release trapped traumas.

Before we even began, he could sense, just from my breathing patterns, that I was carrying suppressed trauma—trauma specifically stored in my root and sacral chakras.

During that intense 90-minute session, he guided me through controlled breathing exercises while applying pressure to specific points on my body.

Rising waves of suppressed feeling erupted. I started to cry uncontrollably as flashes of the elevator event played back in my head. Desperate and afraid, I could see myself sprinting down hallways looking for protection.

My body remembered clearly everything my mind had tried to bury: the uncertainty, the anxiety, the violation I had gone through. Each press on those pressure points triggered another wave of tears.

The specialist explained, *"You've carried these painful feelings deep inside your body and spirit. The root chakra and the sacral chakra are where we store unresolved emotions related to safety, intimacy, and trust."*

As he continued the breathwork, I couldn't stop crying. Memories came back, sharp and clear. The elevator doors, the man's smile, and my frantic escape resurfaced with vivid clarity.

Afterward, I told him, *"I thought I had already worked through this trauma. I can talk about it now without crying or feeling emotional."*

He gently corrected me: *"Yes, your mind has processed the trauma. But your body remembers. The trauma is still stored deep within your physical being, especially in areas like your hips and pelvis. That's why you reacted so strongly during the session."*

Sometimes, because we can discuss it rationally, we believe we have moved past our past. Our bodies, though, tell another tale. Their weight represents our suffering until we are ready to let it go completely.

That session was among the most intense and freeing events of my lifetime. It helped me to realize that healing is a physical as well as a mental or emotional process.

Trauma doesn't just live in our minds. It lives in our cells, our muscles, and our breath. And to truly heal, we must allow ourselves to release it from every part of our being.

· • • ● • ● • • ·

The therapist was helping me understand that even though my conscious mind felt I had healed from past traumas, my body was still carrying that hurt.

He advised reading *The Body Keeps the Score*, which shows how unresolved trauma may linger in the body and, if neglected, might eventually show up as physical problems.

This realization hit me hard—I needed to heal my mind and body. Healing wasn't linear, and I couldn't simply think my way through it.

However, this deep work has already helped me tremendously with grieving Talal. I could now remember fond stories and moments we shared without feeling like I was drowning in sorrow.

The book emphasized that trapped trauma often requires a physical release—through crying, screaming, or even breathwork—rather than suppressing emotions, as I had done for so many years after his passing.

I shared with the therapist how I had cried every day for a year after Talal died, but then, one day, I decided it was *"too much"* and forced myself to stop crying.

In hindsight, I realized that choice wasn't strength but suppression. I had been pushing away emotions my body desperately needed to process.

Talking through it, like I was doing now, was one way I could start letting those emotions flow again and freeing myself from their weight.

"For people who don't believe in a higher spiritual power or religion, how do you think they might let go and find acceptance after experiencing such a loss?" The therapist questioned carefully at one point.

He asked aloud whether ideas like faith in *"what will be, will be"* or submitting to the universe could offer any comfort for someone without a belief in God.

I stopped to give his query much thought before responding. Letting go begins with feeling, I remarked. The emotions cannot be avoided. Before you let them fly, you have to sit with them, let them, and honor them.

• • • ●• • ● • • •

I was reading a book called *Letting Go: The Pathway of Surrender*. It's like my bible for grief. I held up the book to show him. When I first read it with friends, one of them commented that there is no step-by-step instruction manual for how to do this.

"The book taught me that to surrender truly, you must allow yourself to feel the emotions you've been holding onto. But before you can let them go, you must be brave enough to feel them fully," I said, trying to clarify.

When a painful thought arises, you ask yourself, *"What feeling is connected to this thought?"* And instead of pushing it away, you let yourself feel it—without judgment or resistance.

Then you ask yourself, *"Why am I feeling this way?"* And you keep asking *"Why?"* over and over, peeling back each layer until you arrive at the root cause.

"Almost always, that root cause is fear," I explained. *"Fear of loss, fear of pain, or fear of the unknown. Fear lies at the center of it all."*

The therapist nodded thoughtfully. *"Most people are afraid to feel their feelings deeply. They avoid them, suppress them, or distract themselves instead."*

"Exactly. But you can't let go of feelings you've buried. You must lean into them, feel their weight, and allow them to move through you."

For me, doing this inner work made me realize that beneath all my grief and sadness was a core fear—a fear of letting go, of forgetting, of losing the love I felt for Talal.

"And when you feel angry, what's at the bottom of that anger?" he questioned.

I stopped and gave some thought, *"Usually, anger covers depression. And depression sometimes covers fear. Anxiety of change, of loss, of the unknown."*

"So the root is fear?" he asked.

"Yes. At the root of almost every difficult emotion is fear."

"And when you can face that fear, sit with it, and finally let it go, you find a stillness—a peace that's hard to describe," I said. *"That peace came when I surrendered to something greater than myself."*

The therapist leaned forward. *"But what about people who don't believe in a higher power? How can they find that same peace without faith in a divine force?"*

I considered his question. *"That's a tough one. The book suggests that surrender is essential. But if you don't believe in something greater, maybe surrender looks like trusting yourself—trusting the process, trusting life itself."*

"But for me," I continued, *"it was a combination of surrendering to a higher power and doing the deep emotional work. I needed both."*

The therapist nodded, and we sat in silence for a moment. *"Everyone's journey through grief is unique,"* I said. *There's no single right way, but this is what worked for me."*

"I'm still on this journey, and maybe I'll never fully understand why it had to unfold this way. But I trust that there's meaning in it, even if I can't see it yet."

"Healing isn't linear," I added softly. *"But each step forward brings me closer to peace."*

• • • ● • ● • • •

Here's what I would advise you to do if you came to me suffering from trauma.

First, you have to let yourself completely relive and face all the terrible, bad emotions you have been suppressing or dodging.

Don't hide from such feelings. Stay with them regardless of their level of rawness, discomfort, or intensity.

Since this stage is so unpleasant, most individuals skip it. They numb the suffering, divert themselves, or completely ignore it. True healing, then, calls on us to remain present with our emotions and let them rise and flow until they pass.

The secret is not to evaluate your emotions. Just let the feelings come to pass without classifying them as pleasant or bad. Once you really experience things, you can begin to let them go.

But here's the thing—letting go isn't a one-time event. It's a practice. The pain may resurface, and when it does, you'll need to show up for it again and again with patience and compassion for yourself.

I'd also encourage you to ask yourself, *"Why does this hurt so much? What's at the root of this feeling?"*

When I was grieving Talal, I had to ask myself, *"Why can't I let go of the fact that he's gone? Why does this sadness feel like it's become part of who I am?"*

This reflection made me realize something profound: I had tied my identity to Talal. I wasn't just *Dalia*—I was *Dalia and Talal.*

It felt like letting go of my grief would mean letting go of him, and that thought was unbearable. I had unintentionally turned my grief into a way of honoring him, but in doing so, I was preventing myself from living fully.

That realization was a turning point for me.

I wrote about this journey a few days ago: *"It's painful. I wouldn't say I like this situation. But what can I do? It is what it is, and I have to accept it."*

But even as I wrote those words, I realized something else— *"It is what it is"* isn't real acceptance. Those words still carried a subtle undercurrent of anger and resistance.

True acceptance doesn't mean liking what happened. It means making peace with it. It means allowing yourself to feel the pain fully, honoring it, and then repeatedly releasing it.

Healing isn't about erasing the pain. It's about learning to carry it differently, with love and compassion for yourself.

• • • ●•●• • • •

The truth was, I had been clinging to anger and sadness because I thought that's how I could remain loyal to Talal's memory. Deep down, there was guilt—a fear that if I allowed myself to feel happiness again, it would dishonor his death.

I had been avoiding photos of Talal for so long because they brought unbearable pain. Yet, paradoxically, I would forget little details about his face without them. It was a painful cycle of avoidance and longing.

I came to see over time that my self-identity had merged with being *"Dalia without Talal."* My whole sense of self was intertwined around loss, and I couldn't see myself as just Dalia—full and complete on my own.

It took me two decades to recognize that I was keeping myself from living fully in trying to remain loyal to his memory. I wasn't allowing myself to move forward, to heal, or to embrace a life where I could honor him without being consumed by grief.

Real healing started when I started to probe very deeply inside me. Meditating helps one to surface apparently random times of great insight. I would rapidly jot them down in my notebook, catching these ephemeral but strong ideas.

The therapist nodded, *"Those are profound realizations. They show deep self-awareness."*

I had told him before that I needed someone to accompany me to Talal's grave, but I didn't need anyone. The greatest barrier wasn't external—it was internal. It was my fear holding me back.

I was afraid of the tidal wave of emotions that might hit me, what I might feel, and of breaking down completely. Suggesting I needed someone with me was an excuse to avoid confronting those fears head-on.

"You're right," I told the therapist, *"I need to find the courage within myself."*

Healing required a raw and unflinching self-love. It felt like peeling back the layers of an onion—each layer revealing something raw, something vulnerable, something true.

Working through each layer, I began to shift inside. Still, these developments seemed uncomfortable. *"Who am I now?"* I questioned. My priorities changed, my beliefs realigned, and authenticity became my compass—something more vital than social approval or corporate affirmation.

But loving myself wasn't easy. It took courage to forgive myself—for the guilt I carried over not answering Talal's last phone call, for not waving goodbye that final time. I realized I had been holding so much anger toward myself, and that anger had been a wall blocking my healing.

Forgiving myself became the key to unlocking true healing. And from that forgiveness came love—not just for Talal or others, but for myself.

I realized that real love must start within. You cannot pour love into others if your cup is empty. Healing could only truly begin when I learned to love myself—all the messy, imperfect, and tender parts of me.

But, oh, how difficult it was. Self-love isn't something you achieve once and for all—it's an ongoing practice, a daily effort. I remember finishing an especially intense breathwork session and feeling completely overwhelmed. My emotions were so raw and exposed that I couldn't bring myself to talk to anyone. In that moment, I realized that healing isn't always peaceful—it can be exhausting, requiring space to process and rebuild.

Self-love was a journey—one step at a time, one breath at a time. And each step brought me closer to peace.

•　•　•　●　•　●　•　•　•

I stopped, though, and realized that perhaps this challenging moment was meant to be. Though we cannot instantly see it, I think everything occurs for a purpose. Perhaps something significant was scheduled for our conversation today.

I thus choose to let whatever happened pass without evaluating it as either good or harmful. I turned to the experience, knowing that at that very moment, my state of mind and emotions had a reason.

Though family has always been my first concern, I came to see that real authenticity now forms the basis for all else. To show up truly in any aspect of my life, I had to learn to love and accept myself totally.

You can't truly give love to others if you don't love yourself deeply. After Talal's passing, I had carried so much unspoken anger toward myself—anger for not answering his last phone call, for not waving goodbye that final time. That anger had become a heavy barrier, blocking me from grieving and healing.

Looking back, I realize that suppressing my emotions wasn't strength but avoidance. Healing required me to face those difficult feelings head-on, to forgive myself, and to allow love and compassion to flow within me first.

The therapist nodded, his expression kind. *"It's so much easier said than done, though. Loving yourself fully isn't something that happens overnight."*

I gave a small smile. *"No, it's not easy at all. It's one of the hardest things I've ever had to do."* I glanced down briefly before continuing. *"After the trauma release work earlier, I didn't even feel like talking today. But then I reminded myself that everything happens for a reason. Nothing is random. Every moment, every feeling has meaning."*

I met his eyes again. *"I'm still not sure what today's conversation is supposed to reveal, but I'm choosing to stay open to whatever insights come through."*

· · · ●· ● · · ·

The therapist encouraged me to continue at my own pace. I collected my thoughts for a few moments before speaking again, *"You know, that breathing work helped release deeply buried trauma from my body—memories and emotions I thought I had already healed from."*

I paused, my voice trembling slightly. When the practitioner applied pressure to certain areas, emotions locked away for years came flooding out. I was startled by how much my body had been holding onto, even after my mind believed I had processed it.

I wiped away a stray tear. Healing isn't just about the mind; it's about the body, too. This journey of self-love is ongoing. It's about facing those buried emotions, feeling them fully, forgiving myself, and allowing space for growth.

I took a long breath and felt calmness sweep over me. The therapist offered me a friendly, reassuring smile. *"On this road, you have shown great bravery,"* they remarked gently. *"You're on the right road even though the work of self-love and embracing your real self isn't easy."*

I came back, grinning modestly and with thanks. I had great insight and acceptance at that same instant.

By means of this process, I was gradually recovering my actual self—benevolent under tragedy and loss. Every tear dropped, and every challenging feeling I had brought me one step toward my most real self.

This road was no longer only about grieving Talal. It was about mending me—recovering my most brilliant, free form.

Every release brought lightness; every breath came calm; every moment of acceptance drew me toward the core of who I was supposed to be.

Seeing Life After Loss
Rediscovering Purpose and Joy Beyond Grief

*"H*ow are grief and love connected?"* I paused, gathering my thoughts before expressing them.

I think the most natural condition of humans is love. Babies start our lives free of doubt or judgment, full of pure love. Our actual base is that pure, loving state.

But life happens as we develop. Each of our struggles, problems, and demanding relationships sets off feelings ranging from fear to wrath to grief. Our brains then seek to defend us. They stifle these uncomfortable emotions by putting them far down where they go unaddressed.

This suppression occupies the space where love naturally belongs. We must confront these buried emotions to return to our loving, authentic selves. We have to allow them to surface and be fully felt, no matter how uncomfortable or intense they may be.

I paused, feeling the weight of the truth in my words weighing on my mind. *"We can release these emotions—crying if necessary, feeling the hurt, the fear, or whatever comes up—by managing them. Love can only then find its proper place inside each of us."*

Particularly, grief opens the path to this process. It helps us to reestablish our connection with the pure love at our center by softly and lightly enveloping whatever suffering exists. Grieving, therefore, opens room for even greater love to enter our lives.

· • • ● • ● • • ·

When Talal died, I was quite depressed; this loss really troubled me. I went through all the well-known stages of grief—shock, denial, bargaining, anger, and depression.

But those stages weren't neat or linear for me. My emotions overlapped, tangled, and resurfaced when I least expected them. Sometimes, I would be in shock again, even though I had already felt it. Other times, anger and denial would creep back in, pulling me into a loop of bargaining and silent pleas for a different reality.

I was in denial for years, refusing to accept that Talal was truly gone. Anger and sadness became my constant shadows, lingering stubbornly. I even started negotiating—imagining dialogues and secret wishes, begging for an outcome I knew was unworkable.

I carried these strong feelings for nineteen long years. They weighed me down and stopped me from really going ahead since I refused to let myself process or release them totally.

Still, something changed eventually. I stopped resisting over twenty years later. One last time I let myself sit in denial, feel the rough edges of my wrath, and really weep. I let every feeling, unvarnished, free to pass through me.

Something amazing occurred when the storm finally passed. A subdued acceptance swept over me: *"It's okay; I am who I am without Talal in my life now."*

That moment changed everything. It wasn't time that healed me—it was the act of surrendering, of fully feeling everything that had been buried inside me.

For some, acceptance might arrive sooner—it might not wait nineteen years. For me, though, it was a slow, very personal trip, and I had to respect my chronology.

· • • •●•●• • ·

I sank myself into the knowledge of the ego, identity, and core of our actual self during that period.

I came to see that the mind and the heart constitute two forces inside each of us. The mind is the ego, a voice running nearly on autopilot, guiding our behavior and reactions without our conscious knowledge.

For most of our lives, we live in an unconscious condition; the ego guides our decisions and ideas. The ego hooks to roles and titles, persuading us they define us.

"You are a nurse, a mom, a daughter, a friend," it whispers, offering titles that feel comforting and familiar, making us feel secure in our sense of self.

Though comforting, these titles do not really reflect our actual nature. Underneath them is something far more fundamental: *"I am."*

Not a function, title, or presence—a soul.

At our essence, everyone is the same: souls without titles or jobs to balance us out. Still, the ego fights to let go of these labels as it believes they are necessary for survival and approval.

I started one by one removing those identities after I realized this. I released the weight of definitions that no longer helped me.

I began to exist in a simpler state of being—just *being*, without clinging to external validation or labels.

In this state, I could live from the heart rather than being dominated by the ego-driven mind.

I anchored myself firmly in the *now*, in the present moment, free from the chains of past regrets and future anxieties.

Many fail to understand this idea. "*What is she even talking about?*" others would wonder. "*That does not make any sense!*"

Still, it became rather obvious to me. Realizing my actual self beyond labels, roles, and identities was my awakening.

$$\bullet \; \bullet \; \bullet \; \bullet \; \bullet \; \bullet \; \bullet \; \bullet \; \bullet \; \bullet$$

We often define ourselves by our jobs, titles, or money in the bank. These external constructs—built over time—are not who we are at our core.

When we stop attaching our identity to these earthly roles and labels, we open a doorway to our truest selves. Only then can we fully embrace the present moment and the simplicity of life.

For example, when you let go of defining yourself as *"Talal's niece"* or *"Talal's sister,"* you begin to see yourself as an individual soul—separate, whole, and complete.

This is when you give yourself space to *truly grieve* and begin to see loss through a new, transformative lens.

"We need detachment." But detachment doesn't mean withdrawing from life. It means freeing ourselves from the weight of attachments and the illusions they create.

Eliminating these roles and identities leaves a great unanswered question: *"Who am I without all these labels?"*

In that still, free space, long-suppressed ideas and feelings surface. One starts to pay attention to grief, suffering, and unsaid worries.

The beauty of it is that once we let ourselves confront these feelings, they will pass.

Our purest essence, our genuine self, persists.

Many people start this road of self-discovery only after reaching rock bottom. In our worst, most desperate times, we typically welcome change and progress.

The mind rebels when everything seems gone. In that surrender, the soul softly leads us toward greater consciousness and wisdom.

Still, waking up does not always call for catastrophe. It starts sometimes in stillness—through meditation or a period of unbroken tranquility when the heart speaks and the mind quiets.

Meditative techniques can be doors into this deeper consciousness, guiding us inward to reestablish contact with our basic being.

In those times, a great peace floods over us—a tranquility that seems limitless, unquestionable, and timeless.

And after you have tasted it, you will find yourself repeatedly wanting to go back to it.

· · · ● · ● · ● · · ·

Where, thus, does that amazing sense of tranquility originate? It results from a basic yet important insight: at our core, we are all the same.

Deeply, there are no divisions, labels, titles, or separations. Purely, we are just beings—unified, whole, and linked.

This truth is why so many people are drawn to return to that blissful state of oneness. It's not just a fleeting feeling; it's a calling—a pull to reconnect with something eternal and unshakable within ourselves.

When you glimpse this profound truth, it stays with you. You will discover yourself long for going back to that serene, limitless peace.

Many people consider this point to be the start of their trip into greater consciousness. That first taste of inner calm turns into a trigger—a motivation to keep looking inside and strengthening their relationship with themselves.

Still, this trip is quite personal. Two people never follow exactly the same road. Our particular experiences, difficulties, and revelations help us to rediscover ourselves.

Books and teachings about rising consciousness are like roadmaps; they guide you on the proper path. But a map isn't the journey itself.

"It's like reading about how to drive a car; the words alone can't give you the real experience of being on the road."

The journey into higher consciousness requires action, not just knowledge. It demands inner work, dedication, and a willingness to face what lies within.

Teachings and wisdom can guide you, but the real transformation happens when you integrate those lessons into your daily life.

It's beautiful to see so many people embracing this path today. There's a growing awareness—a hunger to truly live in the *now,* free from the noise of the past and the weight of the future.

· · · · ● · ● · · ·

When I finally gave myself permission to grieve Talal's death fully, it wasn't always a safe or comfortable process.

I had to design places purposefully—physical and emotional—where I felt free from expectations, criticism, or judgment. These are places where I can really feel without thinking about being silenced or discounted.

This space was discovered sometimes alone. Alone, I let every feeling—rage, tears, and calm sitting with the rawness of my loss—rise unbounded.

Healing also occurred in front of others at other times—people who could show compassion and nonjudgment. Their presence enabled me to let down my guard, talk honestly, and just myself.

It was essential to feel truly safe in someone's presence. Vulnerability doesn't bloom in spaces clouded by judgment, pretense, or expectation. It requires softness, trust, and acceptance.

"It's so important to have someone who feels like home—someone you can talk to, cry with, and share your grief without fear of being misunderstood or judged."

We all have at least one person like that in our lives. The real challenge is to let them in by lowering our defenses.

I remember a moment that surprised me. Last year, I didn't know *my publisher*, yet I found myself open and vulnerable over the phone.

Setting aside my ego and presenting my real self—raw, honest, unvarnished—part of that vulnerability.

It was quite healing to be seen, held, and embraced in such a place.

Opening myself to my publisher, husband, and closest friends let me unleash years of hidden feelings. It wasn't always easy, but it was necessary.

· · · ●·●·● · · ·

Is there a correlation between having a big ego and low consciousness? Does the ego stand in the way of becoming more conscious?

Yes, the ego thrives in unconsciousness.

Imagine walking down the street and someone bumps into your shoulder. Your first instinctive reaction might be, *"Hey, watch out!"* or *"Be careful!"* That's the ego speaking.

The ego immediately personalizes the event: *"How dare they bump into me? They hurt me and didn't even apologize!"* It takes an unintentional moment and transforms it into an attack on your sense of self.

Even if you respond politely with, *"Excuse me, you hurt me,"* it's still the ego asserting itself, seeking acknowledgment or validation.

But when you're conscious, you respond differently. You become the observer—a witness to your thoughts and emotions rather than being consumed by them.

You seem to have grown a third eye, enabling you to stand back and observe your responses from a distance.

Each of us has an inner voice, that continual stream of ideas passing across our brains. The true question, though, is, "Who *is listening to that voice? Who is the one hearing those thoughts?"*

Thoughts are simply the brain's chatter—noise a protective mechanism generates. But beyond that chatter exists something deeper: a pure consciousness, an inner witness who observes those thoughts without attaching to them or believing them to be absolute truth.

One feels liberated upon realizing this.

Someone once told me, *"I'm so tired of where I am right now."* They stopped then and questioned themselves, *"Wait, who is tired? Who is the 'I' that feels this way?"*

You enter a new level of awareness when you back off and see your ideas like this.

At this level, you begin to realize there's so much more to you than the voice in your head. The brain reacts with emotions—it tries to protect you. But who exactly is the *you* that it's trying to protect?

To answer that, we must dig deeper, peeling away layers of identity, ego, and attachment.

And when we finally reach the core, we encounter a simple, unshakable truth: *"I am."*

Not a title, role, or identity—just *"I am."*

The mind, in its natural role, tries to protect us. It triggers fear, urges us to run, or clings to attachments. But in doing so, it builds walls between us and true consciousness.

We can experience true presence and align with our innermost self by stepping beyond the ego.

· • • ● • ● • • ·

When you're stuck in an unconscious state, grief feels incredibly heavy—overwhelming waves of anger, depression, and a suffocating sense of being trapped in unshakable emotions.

You might think, *"I lost my dear uncle,"* or *"My child got a terrible disease, and I'm so angry at the world for not preventing it."*

Sometimes, anger gets directed outward: *"It's the fault of the person who caused the accident,"* or *"It's the fault of the doctors who couldn't stop this from happening."*

This is how the unconscious mind operates. It searches for someone—or something—to blame. It tries to create logical justifications for the pain because accepting loss feels unbearable.

The ego resists acknowledging that loss often shatters our sense of identity.

When my daughter was diagnosed with type 1 diabetes, my first thought was, *"I've lost my healthy child."* I unknowingly began defining her—and myself—by her condition.

Labels like *mother*, *brother*, or *healthy person* become deeply ingrained. We convince ourselves they represent who we are at our core.

But here's the truth: there's a significant difference between saying, *"I am diabetic,"* and *"I have diabetes."*

When we say, *"I am diabetic,"* we internalize it. It fuses with our identity, becoming an unshakable, permanent label.

But when we reframe it to *"I have diabetes,"* we create space. The condition exists, but it doesn't define who we are.

Research shows that attaching our identity to a label makes it exponentially harder to let go.

Grief operates in much the same way. When we say, *"I lost my uncle, my best friend, my brother,"* those words become anchors, pulling us deeper into loss. A part of us feels as though it died with them.

But when we expand our consciousness, we begin to release those attachments.

"I am no one's daughter. I am me."

Even our names carry weight—they become part of the ego's identity. But beneath those layers, at the deepest level, I am simply a soul—a being existing in the present moment.

Grief isn't purely unconscious or conscious. It's a journey that often begins in unconsciousness but gradually shifts into something more aware and present if allowed.

Through the lens of higher consciousness, I now see grief differently.

The negative emotions—anger, sadness, fear—were faced, processed, and ultimately released. Love has entered their place.

Talal's death marks a chapter in a far more expansive journey than it does merely as a tragedy. His death brought great lessons meant especially for me.

· · ● · ● · ● · · ·

There's a deep belief I hold close to my heart: Talal's death and every experience that followed happened for a greater reason.

I've surrendered to that truth—not out of defeat but of trust. I've surrendered to the trauma of his passing, to my daughter's diagnosis, and to every hardship along the way.

This surrender isn't about giving up; it's about trusting that there's a divine plan—a plan designed not to punish but to guide, heal, and ultimately bring blessings.

I believe Talal's death carried a purpose: to teach me how to live fully in the *now*.

When I look back on the stories his friends have shared and the vivid memories I hold of him, one truth shines through—he was fully present.

Talal had a rare gift. When he spent time with you, he was *there*—completely, wholeheartedly. He listened, he engaged, and he made you feel seen.

"When Talal and I sat together and talked, it felt like we were in our own world. Nothing else existed but that moment."

Others have echoed this sentiment. Talal had a unique way of giving his undivided attention to every person he encountered, and in doing so, he lived entirely in the *now*.

Reflecting on this fills me with profound gratitude. It's not just awareness—it's a deeper acknowledgment of the beauty in each fleeting moment.

"Why did I feel sad for 19 years after Talal died?"

The answer became clear: I hadn't yet learned the lesson his passing was meant to teach me.

The lesson was basic but transforming: to be present—to live totally in *the now*.

Your mind releases its fixation on the past and anxiety about the future when you are really present. You start to watch, to see life as it happens.

Emotions arise, but they pass. They don't linger. They don't weigh you down.

This realization has brought me a peace I can't fully describe, but I know it's real.

I've often referred to Talal as my *"guiding spirit"* because his life and passing have guided me toward this understanding.

Still, even that title—guiding spirit—feels like another attachment—another identity to grab.

I have come to see I have to let go of even that title if I really appreciate his memory.

· · · ● · ● · · ·

I have to be alert to keep present and prevent falling asleep—that is, oblivion. I watch myself all the time, listening for minute signals that my ego could seize.

For instance, it's usually a clue that I've moved out of presence and into ego-driven behaviors when I catch myself using terms like *"me, "my,"* or *"I* excessively.

I'm fortunate to have a close friend who helps me stay awake. During conversations, if he senses I'm drifting into unconscious reactions, he'll gently say, *"Wake up!"*

Here's an example: I might be speaking with my children, and one of them asks me to do something. Should I answer with annoyance or a firm "no"? My friend notes the minute shift in my tone and intensity.

"*Wake up!*" he will remind me. At that instant, I will stop, inhale deeply, and release whatever emotional response was gathering steam. I will concentrate again and go back to being totally present.

This practice isn't something I do once and master—it's an ongoing, moment-by-moment commitment.

Throughout the day, I gently remind myself, "Stay *awake. Stay here. Stay now.*"

Sometimes, the smallest, most ordinary moments catch me off guard. For instance, when I introduce my daughter Leanne to someone, I might say, "*This is my daughter. This is Leanne.*"

It seems harmless, but even in that simple phrase, I notice a possessiveness—a subtle claim of ownership.

"*Why am I calling her my daughter? She's her own person, existing fully in this moment.*"

We live in a world where possessive language feels natural—it's how we communicate. But for me, it's also a trigger, a little signpost reminding me to *wake up.*

To an outsider, my habit of pausing mid-conversation might seem strange. They might think, "*Why does she keep stopping to talk to herself like that?*"

But those little pauses are powerful. They pull me back into the *now.* They help me reset, recenter, and reclaim my presence.

Even though I practice this daily, I'm still human. I still fall back into unconscious patterns. My ego still flares up.

But the difference now is I *notice it*. I catch it, observe it without judgment, and gently guide myself back to presence.

"Okay, there went the ego again. But now I'm back. I'm here."

It's a constant, gentle cycle: observe, notice, release, return.

Each moment offers a chance to begin again—to anchor myself once more in the stillness of *now*.

· · · ● · ● · · ·

I'm at a point in my life where I can't sustain an enlightened state of consciousness 24/7.

I know people who seem to live in a constant state of peace and presence, but I'm not there yet. For me, this journey is ongoing—one that requires patience, dedication, and daily practice.

I still occasionally get pulled into unconscious thinking and reactive behaviors, but the difference now is that I *notice* them. I catch myself in the act and gently guide my awareness back to the present moment.

This journey is deeply personal. It's not about external validation or anyone else's expectations. It's about the quiet, inner work I do within myself.

Mindful breathing is one of the simplest yet most powerful tools I've discovered for staying grounded.

When strong emotions rise—when my ego starts to swell and take over—I can feel it happening in my body.

At those moments, I close my eyes, take a slow, deep breath, and allow the air to fill my lungs. As I exhale, I imagine the breath carrying away my ego, deflating it like a balloon.

Simple conscious breathing helps me to ground, relax, and bring me back to the moment.

Additionally, a great tool on this road has been meditation.

In meditation, the objective is to calm the mind rather than to accomplish something great. It's about releasing the ceaseless flood of ideas and concentrating on something basic, like the natural rhythm of your breath—or perhaps nothing at all.

Stillness meditation, in particular, has been transformative for me.

In this practice, you sit still. You don't move. You don't react, even if a fly lands on your arm. You simply notice its tiny feet on your skin, but you let it be. You just *are*.

I've experienced the purest form of presence in these moments of stillness and silence.

Many great thinkers and teachers have written about living in the present moment. Authors like Joe Dispenza and Eckhart Tolle have been incredible guides for me through their writings. Their works are really worth reading; they have given me tools and ideas that still direct me on this road.

• • • ● • ● • • •

Many people find that their path into present-moment life starts only when they find rock bottom.

For many, it takes a near-death experience, the death of someone close, or an overwhelming catastrophe to stop and declare, *"I can't keep living like this. I need a way out of this agony."*

During those desperate times, the quest starts—not outwards but rather internally. They search for something spiritual, something grounded that cuts across the anarchy of their present existence.

But what they frequently find is a deep change in consciousness, not a straightforward response or outside repair. Anchored in the present moment, they discover silence and tranquility.

Instead of being trapped in regret over the past or paralyzed by anxiety about the future, they learn to anchor themselves in the *now*.

There's something deeply sacred about living fully in the present moment, yet it's nearly impossible to articulate with words. You cannot express it; it is something you have to feel and experience deep within the spirit.

Not everyone will find this road appealing. It is very intimate, usually alone, and calls for great bravery.

For those who choose it, the benefits are almost unrivaled: a quiet that never changes, peace free from conditions, and a clarity that cuts through the ceaseless clamor of the world.

• • • • ● • ● • • •

I've realized something deeply important: many people need a community while walking this path of consciousness.

It's an incredibly tough road to walk alone.

We often return to the world, putting on our *"normal" masks* so we don't stand out, and so people don't think we're strange or different.

Inside, though, our brains are absorbing something so raw and profound that it feels as though we are living in two quite different worlds—the inner world we are silently changing and the outer world we show others.

This is not a simple path. It challenges us to explore layers of past identities and let go of relationships we have kept onto for far too long.

It seems like reincarnation—again and once more—shedding every layer of what we formerly considered characterized us.

And working at this kind of soul level alone can seem almost impossible.

I consider myself to be rather lucky to have a group of folks following this road. We get together weekly in a secure, encouraging environment. We tell our tales, challenges, and successes—no matter how little.

Being around people who understand—who do not criticize, who do not need continual explanations, and who get it—is quite healing.

It's a beautiful experience to feel that connection, to know with certainty that you're *not alone.*

Before Talal passed away, I carried such vivid, beautiful memories of our time together.

I can still picture the tiniest details with startling clarity.

For example, I remember sitting beside him in the car—how his hands rested on the steering wheel before gently sliding down to the gearshift.

They're such ordinary moments, yet they're etched in my memory as if they happened just yesterday.

His smile still sparkles, his eyes show warmth as he listens, and his fingers move naturally across his guitar strings.

I carry with me these times. With time, they haven't faded. They still live vibrantly and are extremely meaningful—a subdued reminder of love and presence.

· · · ● ● · ● ● · ·

These are the kinds of memories that come flooding back to me now.

But something has shifted. These memories no longer bring sadness, pain, or anger. Instead, they are wrapped in pure, open-hearted love and gratitude.

When I reflect on these snapshots of Talal's life, my heart feels full and open.

"Thank you, God," I whisper softly. *"Thank you for bringing these memories back to me, memories I thought were lost or buried deep inside. Thank you for these beautiful messages."*

The most profound message I've received from this journey is the importance of letting go of attachments.

Attachments—to identities, to roles, to expectations—do not define who I truly am.

To find true freedom, I must connect to the inner light within me—the essence of my being—beyond anything fleeting or external.

Each of us carries a divine light within. Some call it God, others refer to it as a higher self, and some see it as the core of their true being.

If connecting to a higher power outside yourself feels distant or impossible, that's okay.

Instead, look inside. Your heart and spirit have a holy light just waiting for you to find again.

On this path, treat yourself gently. Demand neither forced results nor perfection.

Let yourself feel whatever comes up—joy, grief, or wrath.

If you feel like crying, let yourself cry. If anger bubbles up, don't suppress it—let it flow through you.

Heavy emotions are like passing storms—they come, pour, and then move on.

But here's the truth: You are not your emotions. You are the steady, peaceful presence seeing them come and leave.

You build a holy place inside yourself where healing, love, and peace can enter freely when you let emotions run unhindered by judgment or opposition.

• • • ● • ● • • •

Something quite amazing happens when you design that open area inside. One starts to feel a great sense of love and tranquility.

This is an incomprehensible sensation—one you might have had in brief quiet times when everything seemed exactly aligned and whole.

Think of your heart expanding out like a flower in full bloom, its petals softly unfolding under the sun's warmth.

You feel a soft, glowing warmth spreading across your chest, accompanied by a light, tingling sensation. At that moment, energy flows freely—no blocks, no resistance, just pure openness.

You might even think, *"My heart feels so beautifully open right now."*

Because that's precisely what's happening—you're experiencing pure, unconditional love. Love for yourself, for others, and for all of existence.

This love isn't conditional. It doesn't depend on circumstances, validation, or expectations. It's expansive, boundless, and universal—a love that asks for nothing in return.

But this kind of love begins with *you.*

It starts with fully accepting yourself—every strength, flaw, and hidden part of your being—without judgment or shame.

It's about seeing yourself through the lens of unconditional love as if you're looking into the eyes of your truest, most authentic self.

Whether you call it God, Spirit, Source, or simply the quiet power within you, the key is always the same: *go inward.*

Observe yourself with tenderness instead of harsh criticism.

Let life unfold gently within you without resistance. Allow the armored layers to peel away, one by one, revealing the radiant core that has been there all along.

This is the path to inner peace. It's the journey to boundless love.

And it's a journey of saying *yes* to yourself—again and again, with each breath, each moment, and each choice.

· · · ● · ● · ● · · ·

This book journey has taken me down a path I never anticipated.

When I first began writing, I told my publisher that this wasn't supposed to be about me. I said it was meant to be about Talal—honoring his memory and preserving his beautiful legacy. But somewhere along the way, something shifted. As I worked through the chapters, I found myself removing entire sections of what I had originally written. It no longer felt aligned with the deeper purpose emerging through the words.

This book isn't just about Talal—it's about the larger journey his life and passing set me on. It's about the path I've been walking to uncover meaning, embrace consciousness, and experience true healing.

While I can share my journey and offer guidance, I recognize this path is deeply personal. It's not a one-size-fits-all map.

I've come to believe that every hardship I endured had a divine purpose. Every loss and struggle shaped me for this moment.

My publisher and I have discussed how God communicates with us through people, seemingly ordinary objects, and life experiences.

Maybe I was meant to experience the loss of Talal and all the trauma that followed so that my story could serve as a glimmer of light for others navigating their own darkness.

It's true—how could I hope to guide others toward healing if I hadn't been healed myself?

As I sit here reflecting, gratitude is the emotion that rises most strongly—gratitude to God and to every person who supported me during those 19 long years of grief.

Today, I feel healed—healed from Talal's passing, healed from my daughter's diabetes diagnosis, and healed from countless other wounds I've carried along the way.

I've reached a place of inner peace. I see the world differently now, which may mean I've reached a point where I can gently guide others along their healing paths, not as an expert with all the answers, but as someone who's walked this road and can now point the way.

I can point toward the moon so others might see its brightness, but I cannot be the moon itself.

This travel is not about reaching some ideal location. It's about never stopping to grow, learn, and gently remove one by one layer of consciousness.

Every instant of this trip will have been worthwhile if I can use the knowledge I have to guide others still negotiating their own darkness.

Moments and Experiences Live Forever

Keeping Their Spirit Alive Through Memory

Talal died at just 19, while I was twenty-one. The jolt ripped up my universe. Death seemed to me always something reserved for elderly people, not for someone as youthful and vibrant as Talal.

He was vivid, honest, and unreserved in taking chances. His untimely loss made me face a hard reality: death does not discriminate by age; it can strike anyone at any moment.

I felt a great degree of betrayal in the aftermath. This was not the way life was meant to play out. Young people with unlimited opportunities ahead of us. But within the suffering, I discovered a lesson I carry with me today: life is brittle, and none of us are assured of tomorrow. Something like this worries me since it may happen to my brothers or me.

Talal's absence started to teach me something very deep over time. The most valuable lesson concerned really being present with people. Rather than being fixated on the pain of those we have lost, I came to see we should value the times we spent with others still living. When it might be the last time we laugh, eat, or even have a basic chat with someone we love is a question we never know. However, this means living with thanks for every moment you share—not with anxiety over loss.

Talal effortlessly embodied this lesson. When he was with his friends, he was *with* them—no phones, no distractions. When he played guitar with me, there was nothing else in the world except our music.

I try to mirror that in my life now. I tell myself to calm down, pay great attention to the people I am with, and listen intently.

It is not always easy to be totally present. There are several directions life pulls us in, and distractions abound. I have to remind myself very often to slow down and really see the surroundings.

Sometimes, all it takes is sipping a cup of coffee. I concentrate on the warmth of the mug in my hands, the strong scent developing with every drink, and the smooth flavor lingering. Many times, these little events we hurry through become anchors dragging us back into the present.

It's been twenty years since Talal passed away, but his memory continues to guide me. He taught me to approach life with an open heart and to show love freely and deeply. I hope people remember me that way for what I did and how I made them feel.

Losing Talal was one of the hardest experiences of my life, but it gave me a profound gift: the determination to live fully and love deeply. Now, when I drive past the place where he died or step into his old bedroom, I don't feel weighed down by sadness but a sense of peace and a quiet gratitude for the lessons he left behind.

I carry those lessons daily, trying to honor his legacy through kindness, presence, and love.

• • • ● • ● • • •

Talal's capacity for total presence in every moment was among the most amazing qualities about him. He was really there—no phone in hand, no distractions dragging him away—in conversation, in a quiet time, on a guitar session. When you were with him, it seemed as though the rest of the world vanished.

I have carried forward this lesson—a dedication to being there, to really listening, and to allowing people around me to feel noticed and valued. I now approach shared meals, chats, or quiet times with the same attention Talal shows.

Not always simple is what it is There are many directions life pulls us in and distractions abound. But when I stop, inhale, and concentrate on the person or work ahead of me, I feel as though one moment at a time Talal's lessons are being carried forward.

This mindfulness honors Talal and the way he lived his life, not only as a habit. This mindfulness has become more than just a habit—it's a tribute to Talal and the way he lived his life.

Motivated by Talal, I started working toward the same. I concentrated on being present with those still here rather than buried in ideas about his disappearance. It wasn't—and still isn't—always easy. But I keep working at it because I know how much it matters.

I remember a conversation with someone who gave me beautiful advice. She said, "When *you pick up a cup of coffee, watch your hand reach for it, feel your fingers wrap around it, notice how you lift it, feel the cup's warmth against your lips, and savor the taste of each sip."*

Her words made me realize how often I had been moving through life on autopilot—eating, drinking, and even talking without truly noticing what I was doing.

I now aim to taste every bite of my food, really enjoy it, and occasionally consider its beginnings. *These tomatoes were grown by someone? From which farm did they travel? Their route to my plate was what?*

This basic mindfulness exercise lets me slow down and enjoy the richness of daily events. It's a little yet significant approach to pay tribute to Talal.

· · · **·** · **·** · · ·

Practicing mindfulness has become a form of meditation for me—a way to quiet the noise in my mind and stay rooted in the present moment. I'm learning to carry this approach into my everyday life.

When talking with someone, I listen to their words and everything they express. I notice their body language, tone, and the feelings behind their statements. When you are totally present, it is amazing how much you can observe.

Even in silence, occasionally, one can see emotions written on someone's face. You pick up their little pauses in speech, the flutter of gloom in their eyes, or the friendliness of their grin. At that point, you are truly present for someone—not only listening but also comprehending them.

This change of viewpoint has affected my experience of the planet. Food tastes richer, colors seem more vivid, and interactions seem to delve deeper. Every moment seems more alive, as though I have moved from viewing life in black and white to experiencing it in full color.

Naturally, it is not always simple. Phones buzzing, never-ending chores, and transient ideas dragging me away from the now abound in the world as diversions. But once I have experienced its effectiveness, I keep going back to this practice. When I am totally in life, I realize how great it feels.

This journey has let me realize something very important: small events count just as much in life as the major ones. The warmth of your morning coffee, the sound of a friend laughing, or the golden shine of the sun on your skin—the threads that weave a significant existence are those ones.

Considering these little, sometimes missed events has changed my viewpoint. I now see how many amazing events are strewn over every day.

I am still developing this knowledge and application. I battle to stay present some days; other days it comes naturally. Still, I am always appreciative of this gift—that which allows me to see and experience the world—regardless of how well I manage.

It has altered my life, my love, and my interactions with others. And in those quiet, deliberate times, I feel near to Talal—as though I am living the way he always knew we were supposed to.

• • • • ● • ● • • •

This past year has been an inward journey—a deep exploration of my heart and mind. I realized I had buried many of my feelings about Talal, locking them away because they were too heavy to face.

Those emotions, nonetheless, did not go. They stayed with me, silently influencing me in ways I never completely understood. Though it wasn't easy, I felt Talal's presence with me through it all, almost as if he walked me through each phase. His passing became a turning point in my life, molding me into the person I am now, not only a tragic accident.

I still don't have all the answers about what I want for my future, but one thing is clear: I want to be remembered as someone with an open heart, like Talal. He had a beautiful way of deeply caring for everyone around him, and I want to carry that same light forward.

Having an open heart isn't about avoiding pain or pretending everything is okay. It's about allowing yourself to feel—deeply and honestly.

Sadness, anger, joy—every emotion has its place. You must let yourself experience them fully and then let them go. That's how real peace begins.

• • • • ● • ● • • •

This journey of openness has taught me that being vulnerable isn't a weakness; it's a strength. And in those quiet moments of acceptance, I find myself closer to Talal—his kindness, courage, and unwavering love for others.

I lately thought about how readily we grow attached to objects—the houses we live in, the cars we drive, the items we collect. None of that counts, though, when someone dies.

Their wealth or position eludes us. We recall their showing of love, their making of us, and their bringing of kindness into the planet. Those are the things our hearts carry.

We still have time to do good, love sincerely, and leave behind a legacy of compassion and care—a basic but significant truth. How we treat others and how much we care for them determines our value rather than what we own.

But we have to start with ourselves if we are to really love and look after other people. If your own cup is empty, you cannot pour love into another. Self-love isn't selfish—it's necessary. It's about nurturing your heart and mind to freely give to those around you.

When I think about Talal, I see that this is his legacy and a sobering reminder of how brief our stay here is. Our best bet is to make every moment count and every relationship significant.

When we consider legacy, we often picture great accomplishments or obvious success. But true legacy isn't measured by what we accomplish—it's found in the love, wisdom, and light we leave behind in the hearts of others. Talal's legacy is one of love, faith, and connection.

Faith was a core part of Talal's identity, even at a young age. His love for God wasn't rigid or bound by rules; it was pure, deep, and personal. He wanted everyone around him to experience that same connection.

Talal, just 19, knew things many people spend a lifetime looking for. His words, deeds, and soft demeanor left a legacy still guiding me now.

Talal left behind love—love for God, others, and oneself. It lives on in the stories people share about him, in how they remember how he made them feel. After all these years, people still talk about his kindness, warmth, and caring for others.

I try to honor Talal by living as he did—with an open heart and a deep connection to faith. It's not always easy, but I know it's the best way to carry his light forward. In doing so, I hope to pass on some of his wisdom to others.

When I think of Talal, the first thing that comes to mind is his deep love for God. At the time, this felt unusual to me. He was a teenage boy full of life and laughter, yet his faith was constant and unwavering. It wasn't about following rules—it was about trust, connection, and a quiet inner peace.

I discovered an email from Talal shortly after his passing. It was sent a week before he died, but I hadn't noticed it until much later. When I first tried to open it, the message was corrupted—filled with strange symbols and unreadable text. For nearly twenty years, I couldn't access it.

But two months ago, while seated quietly in Talal's old room in my grandfather's house, I checked my old inbox again. And there it was—the same email, clear and intact this time. The subject line read, "Love *of God.*"

In his message, Talal spoke about finding peace and love through faith. It wasn't about rituals or routines—it was about trust, connection, and a quiet inner peace. He wrote with clarity and purpose, encouraging me and his sisters to seek a deeper connection with God, to root ourselves in love, and to find strength through trust.

Reading his words, Talal seemed to be addressing me personally. He seems to have left behind a guide to negotiate loss and find comfort in religion, a treasure map. His voice felt close, and his comments stuck with me long after I closed the email.

"Remember I'm here whenever you're sad," he had said during his last days. It was basic yet significant—words that seemed to span time, as though he had expected the depth we would need them for.

Talal's last email was more than just a note; it was a gift. Preserved in words, a bit of his heart reminds me to convey his legacy of love, faith, and connection.

· • • ●• • ● • •· ·

This experience helped me to understand how very unique Talal was. He was quite young, but he carried a knowledge of love and faith that seemed much beyond his years.

I now try to live with an open heart and a faith based on connection and trust, carrying his message with me instead of rituals.

His faith wasn't heavy with rules or restrictions. It was light, warm, and deeply personal—like speaking to a trusted friend.

I remember a moment he shared with someone close to him. Talal said: *"If we want to be together forever, we need to focus on God first."*

He truly believed that love rooted in faith was enduring, something that transcended even death.

Talal's link to his faith then still eluded me completely. I got worried because he was getting too serious and reflective for someone his age. Still, I see how mistaken I was now. Talal had found something deep that brought him love, peace, and direction instead of distance or restriction. His faith permeated all he did, every interaction he had, every word he spoke; it was not something apart from his personality.

Talal still guides me even now when I consider those last notes. His words are a quiet lighthouse guiding me through periods of uncertainty and anxiety. Talal left behind a legacy of the heart, far more than just memories, by means of his faith and love. Talal passed away at just 19 years old, which is remarkable. Most people spend their lifetime trying to comprehend the kind of love, faith, and wisdom he seemed to have inherently. He understood something profound: *loving God can help us love ourselves and others more deeply.* It's a lesson that stays with me every day.

When I think of Talal now, I feel a mix of sadness and gratitude. I feel sad because he's no longer here and grateful because he left behind such an incredible gift—a legacy of love, faith, and kindness.

His words, deeds, and messages led to the same truth: peace results from the relationship with God, ourselves, and others. I sense his presence even now when I go back over his last words. As though he were still here, his love and wisdom still guide me gently, reminding me of what really counts.

I wish I had understood Talal's depth better when he was alive. But even now, his legacy remains a source of strength and comfort. Whenever I feel lost or overwhelmed, I return to his words about love and faith.

It's as though Talal left behind a lantern, its light still glowing softly, showing me the way forward.

$$\bullet \; \bullet \; \bullet \; \bullet \; \bullet \; \bullet \; \bullet \; \bullet \; \bullet \; \bullet$$

When I think about Talal's final messages, I feel a gentle warmth—a glow that stays with me. One message stands out in particular: *"We'll come back together when we let go and focus on God."* It felt like he understood something about love that most people desperately try to grasp.

At Talal's funeral, someone close to him shared something unforgettable. She said, "I *got his last message saying he'd always be here when I'm sad. So I just felt he was with me."* Her words sent a shiver through me. In his quiet wisdom, Talal seemed to know he was heading away. Still, he left words of comfort and assurance instead of fear so that those he loved would know his presence long after he was gone.

My world seemed to have darkened totally when Talal passed away. Without him, I could not see life continuing forward. I felt I had embraced what happened for almost twenty years. I felt I had atoned for the death. Deep down, though, I still clung to the hurt, the grief, and even a little resentment. Those emotions stayed with me, gently influencing my decisions and daily life.

Afterwards, something changed. I came to see that clinging to my grief was not benefiting anyone—not Talal, not the people in my vicinity, most certainly not me. Letting go did not mean I was bidding Talal farewell. It didn't mean I loved him any less. It simply meant I was permitting myself to heal.

For years, I had seen myself as Talal's niece, his best friend, and someone carrying the weight of his loss. But that's not all of who I am. I had to learn that I could honor Talal while being completely myself—whole, present, and unburdened by loss. Though it was a difficult lesson, it also released something. And I try to live with that same mild acceptance every day, carrying Talal's light ahead in my path.

Something incredible happened when I finally allowed myself to let go and face the weight of my grief. Even after twenty years, Talal is still teaching me.

People often say that when someone dies, their lessons end—that they've taught you everything they could while alive. But with Talal, it feels different. His lessons continue, shaping me in unexpected ways.

To continue learning from him, I had to confront all the feelings I had buried for so long—sadness, anger, confusion, and even guilt. It wasn't easy, and facing those emotions felt like reopening old wounds, but something beautiful happened in the process.

Working through every feeling, my viewpoint started to change. When I considered Talal, instead of drowning in grief, I saw our time together as something valuable—like seeing a great movie from beginning to end. Every memory seemed vivid, every lesson obvious, and every moment bursting with love.

The past does not now weigh me down. Rather, I see it from a higher vantage point, more peacefully and clearly. I feel as though I have been handed a fresh set of eyes that allow me to find beauty in formerly only painful situations.

This shift has changed how I remember Talal and how I see the world around me. I've learned to step back from overwhelming emotions and view things with a calmer heart. This doesn't mean I don't feel sadness—it just means it no longer defines the memory.

Talal is still here in every lesson, reflection, and moment of clarity he's gifted me. His presence continues to guide me gently but firmly, like a quiet compass pointing me back to love, faith, and peace.

Talal's final gift to us wasn't tangible—it was far more enduring. He taught us to love deeply and let go gracefully when the time came.

He showed me that loving God creates a bridge to loving others better, with more patience, kindness, and understanding. Even though he's no longer here, his lessons continue to guide me every single day.

Sometimes, I wish I could sit with Talal and tell him how much he's still teaching me. But deep down, I believe he knows. I feel it in the quiet moments—when I'm at peace, when I'm kind to someone, or when I find strength in vulnerability. In those moments, it feels like Talal's light is shining through me, continuing to make the world just a little bit better.

When I think of Talal, one of my strongest memories is of his guitar. We used to sit together on my bed, each holding our guitar, and he would patiently teach me how to play. I can still see his fingers dancing over the strings as he showed me the chords for Metallica's *Nothing Else Matters.*

I couldn't bear looking at a guitar long after he passed away. The sight of it brought a sharp, aching sadness that felt impossible to carry. Frustration and loss drove me even to break out my guitar. I stopped completely listening to Metallica.

Time has, however, softened those lines. Hearing *Nothing Else Matters,* I find myself back in those quiet afternoons. I almost feel the soft bed under me, hear his soft voice guiding me through each note, and see his concentrated face as he plays.

And those memories now make me smile rather than cry. Talal seems to be right next to me, guitar in hand, reminding me of the delight we experienced at those times.

• • • ● • ● • • •

So many little things remind me of Talal—small moments, everyday objects, fleeting expressions.

I have his picture displayed in my house, and every time I walk past it, I say a quiet hello in my mind. It's a simple habit, but it makes me feel connected to him, as though he's still part of my daily life.

Sometimes, when I'm talking to someone, and they smile in a shy, familiar way, I see Talal's face in that expression. It's fleeting, just a moment, but it feels like he's saying, *"I'm here!"* through that person's smile. These moments feel like tiny, precious messages sent just for me.

The road between Khobar and Riyadh carries its weight in my heart. That's where Talal died. For years, driving on that road filled me with dread. The sadness and fear would settle deep in my chest, and every mile felt heavy.

But with time, something evolved. I get an unexpected calm when I travel that road. Once intolerable, the same length of asphalt has turned rather beautiful. I appreciate the change, even though I'm not sure exactly why.

Talal died at one particular place—about two hours from Khobar. Every time I got ready to approach it, I would brace myself. My heart would rush with anxiety while my hands would tighten on the steering wheel. Now, though, as I get close to that location, I experience something quite different. As if Talal were here, whispering, *"It's okay,"* a great calm sweeps over me. I'm present.

Though I can't quite articulate it, I keep it close as a reminder that peace can still find its way through, even in places defined by loss.

Ramadan always brings Talal to mind. He loved this sacred month, and it feels fitting—and deeply bittersweet—that he passed away during it.

His 20th death anniversary is just two days away. Two decades have passed, yet it feels like both a lifetime and a moment. Time has a strange way of folding in on itself when it comes to grief.

Family gatherings also remind me of Talal. He loved those moments of togetherness—laughter filling the room, conversations stretching late into the night. Whenever we're all together, I can almost feel him there with us, a quiet presence in the middle of our joy.

And then there's *Paris.* The word itself brings his mother to mind. She lives there now, and every mention of the city feels like a bridge connecting us to her and him.

I visited Talal's old room in my grandfather's house a few months ago. The room felt frozen in time, a quiet monument to his memory. As I touched his old belongings and flipped through baby pictures, I felt a deep sense of closeness, as though he was right there.

While browsing through his things, I found a large book about Paris. When I opened it, I discovered a handwritten note from Talal's mother on the first page. She had copied a poem by Khalil Gibran about how our children are not truly ours—they belong to God.

Reading those words made my chest tighten. I thought of Talal's mother and the great grief she would be carrying. Simultaneously, though, I was overwhelmed with thanks for our time with Talal, the love he bestowed upon us, and the way his spirit lingers in quiet areas of our life.

Even though he's no longer here, the love he shared remains. It's something we carry with us—a legacy far more enduring than any physical presence could ever be.

My memories of Talal are like a mosaic—small, vivid pieces that come together to form a picture of his life. The guitar lessons, his shy smile, the road where he left us, Ramadan gatherings, family moments, and even the book about Paris are all fragments of him that I hold close.

Sometimes, these memories bring a sting of sadness, but more often, they leave me feeling grateful. I am grateful that I had the chance to know, learn from, and love him. Even in memory, I am grateful that his presence still feels alive.

I've realized that remembering someone we've lost doesn't always have to be filled with sorrow. It can also be beautiful, like hearing a favorite song unexpectedly or finding peace during a quiet drive.

Talal isn't physically here, but he continues to teach me every day. He's teaching me to find beauty in the places where grief once lived, to keep loving deeply, even when it hurts, and to hold onto moments of connection, no matter how fleeting. For that, I'll always be thankful. Talal's love and wisdom are still here, stitched into the fabric of my life, reminding me of what truly matters.

A deep ache settles in my chest whenever I think about Talal's mother. The weight of her loss is something I can't fully comprehend. She was not with him in his last hours, and I sometimes wonder how she managed to get on.

Losing a child has to feel like a soulful, intolerable fracture. Maybe the only way to get through it is to keep in mind that our children belong to God, and we are privileged to be looking after them for a little period. They are not really ours.

When I found Talal's last email two months ago, his words stayed with me. In it, he spoke about the importance of being close to God and finding love and peace through that connection. That email wasn't just a message but a reminder—a map left behind for us to follow.

Talal was deeply spiritual, but his faith wasn't about rules or rituals. It was about connection, trust, and love. He shared that with everyone around him, not by preaching but by living as an example.

I'm not someone who will stand on a platform and preach, but I've felt a shift within myself this year. My connection to God feels more personal and alive. In a way, that feels like honoring Talal—continuing the legacy he started.

Faith isn't always loud; sometimes, it's quiet. Sometimes, it's just a moment of stillness, a whispered prayer, or a feeling of peace. And in those moments, I feel close to Talal, as though he's still guiding me forward.

Talal dreamed of becoming a doctor to treat illnesses and care for people with genuine love and compassion. For him, healing wasn't just about medicine but about kindness, connection, and empathy.

Even at a young age, his compassionate nature made a difference in many lives. Stories about how Talal made people feel seen, valued, and loved still abound from my cousins, friends, and even my dad. These tales attest to his subdued but potent influence on people around him.

In my way, I've tried to carry that spirit forward. As a nurse, I help people heal physically and emotionally. And sometimes, it's not about my job—it's about being there for someone who needs a listening ear, a comforting word, or simply someone to sit with in pain.

Writing this book feels like an extension of that same calling. It's another way to honor Talal and keep his spirit alive in the stories I share and the reflections I uncover.

When I started writing about Talal, I thought I was trying to preserve his memory. I didn't fully understand what that meant. But as I dug deeper—through conversations, old memories, and moments of raw vulnerability—I began to see the bigger picture.

Talal's legacy isn't just about remembering him; it's about continuing his work in whatever form. I try to do this through caregiving, writing, and the quiet, intentional acts of kindness I try to bring into the world every day.

In those moments, I feel Talal's presence with me, as though he's walking alongside me, still guiding my steps.

This journey, filled with love, loss, and reflection, taught me much. I'm deeply grateful for my path and the people God has placed in my life. Even the hardest moments, the ones I thought I'd never survive, have shaped me into the person I am today.

I've come to believe there's a larger plan at work, even if it's unclear. Talal's death, as painful and senseless as it felt, was somehow part of that plan. It's hard to accept, but it brings me peace.

Talal wanted to heal people and dreamed of becoming a doctor. In my own way, I've carried on that dream as a nurse. We both wanted the same thing—to help, comfort, and make people feel better. It's a shared path, even if we're no longer walking it side by side.

I hear many stories about Talal from cousins, friends, and even my father. I am amazed at how deeply he touched people's lives in his short time here. They talk about how he was always there for them and how he made them feel seen and valued. These stories warm my heart, and in those moments, it feels as though Talal's kindness is still here, echoing through the lives he touched.

In my work as a nurse, I often think of Talal. Healing isn't just about medicine or medical procedures—it's about being there for someone when they're scared, listening when they need to talk, and offering comfort when words fail.

Talal would have been an incredible doctor—not just because of his knowledge, but because of his heart. And in my own way, I try to carry that same heart into the work I do every day.

Maintaining Talal's legacy calls for living in a way that honors who he was, not only for remembering him. It is about using my actions to carry his love, compassion, and kindness into the world.

I feel like I'm carrying on what Talal started when I look after a patient, listen to a friend who is struggling, or provide someone who needs it a moment of comfort.

This book has become another way for me to share his message. Through its pages, I say, *"Look at Talal's life. Look at his heart. Let's all try to carry a little bit of that light with us."*

I'm doing it in my way, through my words and work, but I know it's something Talal would be proud of.

Sometimes, I pause to think about how Talal and I still follow the same road even if we are not side by side. We both wanted to heal people—their bodies, hearts, and spirits.

I stay near him for this common goal. Across time and distance, this is a silent, unspoken link. And in those times, I most sense Talal's presence—as though he were right next to me, guiding each step.

• • • • ● • ● • • •

Writing this book has been a discovery, reflection, and healing journey. Through sharing these stories, I've understood Talal's legacy in a way I didn't before.

Talal's presence isn't just in the past—it's woven into the lives he touched and the love he left behind. Honoring him means living with the same kindness and compassion he carried every day.

When I began this book, I thought I understood what I was trying to do. But looking back, I realize I was stepping into something much larger than I expected. It was like trying to put together a puzzle, knowing nothing about the final image.

I had to sit with memories that hurt as well as were lovely. I had to speak with family members, friends, and even those who had quick but significant interactions with Talal from many perspectives.

It was not straightforward. Some days seemed like sorting through a box of strong emotions, and I wasn't always sure I could keep on. Still, the bits began to fit one another gradually.

Talal's legacy started to seem to me like a torch he handed me, a light I could carry forward from the past.

And now, with every word I write, every patient I tend to, and every act of kindness I offer, I feel like I'm holding that torch high, trying to light the planet like Talal once did.

This trip has felt like negotiating a meandering road with surprising bends, steep climbs, and amazing vistas. Looking back, I feel profoundly grateful to God for guiding me along this path, even when the way forward wasn't clear.

It's strange how time has given me a new perspective. It's as though I've been handed a fresh pair of glasses that let me see the world with more clarity and compassion. Things that seemed random or pointless today seem like well-placed stepping stones guiding me to where I am now.

God has set amazing people on my path throughout my life. Whether they stayed for a season or a lifetime, every person contributed to my development, recovery, and forward motion. However, at the time, I could not see it; every interaction, lesson, and moment had significance.

Twenty years ago, Talal passed away, and it felt as though my whole life had collapsed. Everything appeared to be out of control, and I found it impossible to see how life might proceed. But over time, I have come to see that Talal's death was a key landmark on a larger map God created.

It does not imply that the loss caused any less suffering. Now, though, I see how that terrible event turned into a turning point on a new road lined with purpose, love, and a closer relationship with myself and others.

Life seems to me like a story. Every chapter—regardless of its content—joy, loss, or quiet times of contemplation—serves a function. Every moment is a necessary component of the story that shapes our larger life narrative.

Though it came from a place of grief, I am appreciative of this understanding. It has shaped and strengthened me and allowed me to see beauty where I once only saw pain.

This journey has changed the way I see life. Now, when I face something difficult or painful, I remind myself that it might be leading me somewhere meaningful—just like Talal's passing, which was as devastating as it was, eventually led me to where I am today.

It doesn't erase the sadness or make the pain less real, but it gives me hope that something good might quietly take root even in the hardest moments.

Writing this book has felt like stumbling upon a calm, quiet refuge amid a raging storm. When I began this journey, my life felt like it was falling apart.

I had moved away from my family—my parents, my brothers, everyone I had grown up with—and discovered myself alone in the vast city of Riyadh. There was a lot of isolation. Just me in an unknown location; no family nearby, no close friends. I felt as though I had dropped all behind.

As if that weren't enough, life delivered another blow: we discovered something was wrong with my daughter.

It felt like I had fallen into a deep, dark hole with no way out. The weight of it all seemed unworkable. Uncertain whether I would ever surface, I let myself sink into that gloom and loneliness for a while. Then, something quite unanticipated occurred. I let go in my lowest hour. I gave God a whisper, "*Okay, I give up. You take over.*"

It was like letting the current carry me while I relaxed on the brink of a riverbank. I gave up trying to run everything and stopped battling the flow. And something wonderful happened in that surrender: peace.

It didn't change my circumstances. My problems did not vanish on demand. Still, something changed within me. I had a great calm in my chest, a stillness not experienced in years.

I asked myself, "*Where did this peace come from? Why, given everything is still so difficult, do I feel so calm?*"

It was a flash of insight—a realization that occasionally, peace cannot result from mending the surrounding brokenness. It results from letting go and believing that we are being carried somewhere safe, even though we cannot yet see the destination.

The more I reflected, the more I felt connected to something greater than myself—a force, a presence, a light quietly guiding me all along.

I discovered a light within me that I hadn't known was there. It wasn't loud or blinding but gentle, steady, and warm. That light enabled me to begin releasing years of guilt, anger, and sadness—burdens I had carried for so long. I started to forgive slowly, first of all myself, then of others.

Every step and every moment of release let my heart create more space for love.

Looking back, I can see the reason behind every fight. Every issue, every heartbreak, every dark moment felt like a stepping stone gently guiding me to where I am now.

I'm thankful for all of it—the good and the bad, the joyful and the painful. Because without them, I wouldn't have found this version of myself.

I feel genuinely excited about what comes next for the first time in a long while. I know there will still be hard days, but I also know that good things are often hidden in places we least expect them. Sometimes, they don't look like blessings at first, but they become clear over time. I feel genuinely excited about what comes next for the first time in a long while. I know there will still be hard days, but I also know that good things are often hidden in places we least expect them. Sometimes, they don't look like blessings at first, but they become clear over time.

It's strange how writing about Talal—his life, his love, his lessons—has taught me so much about myself. His story became a mirror, reflecting the parts of me I had forgotten, the strengths I didn't realize I carried.

Through his story, I discovered calm among turmoil. I discovered that if you're ready to look closely enough, there is always something beautiful waiting to be found, even if life seems unbearably heavy and completely messy.

When I consider the beginning of my path, one central concept comes to me: letting go. It's like when you at last set down a large, weighty backpack.

Looking back to where this trip started, I find one recurring motif: letting go. It's like dragging an infinitely weighty backpack for miles, feeling every ounce of its weight, then laying it down.

But letting go isn't always straightforward. What exactly was I letting go of? For me, it was about surrender. I was handing over my fears, grief, and endless need for control to God.

For others, it might be different. Some might call it trusting the universe, science, or even the inherent goodness within themselves. The fundamental truth, though, is still the same: it's about realizing everything is being held together by something more than ourselves.

It reminds me of learning to swim. Originally afraid of sinking, you thrash and flail. Eventually, though, you come to see that if you trust and relax, the water can hold you. When you stop fighting the current, you discover a sense of calm, even in the deepest waters.

I thought you had to hit rock bottom for the longest time to learn this lesson. I believed you had to fall into a deep, dark hole to understand the power of letting go.

And it's true: rock bottom feels horrible. The silence is deafening; the air feels weighty. Then, something amazing occurs. In the middle of the blackness, you begin to see minute flashes of light. Small sparks. Like fireflies dispersed over a thick forest.

Though brief, those sparks are sufficient to point you ahead. They serve to remind you that even here, there is still beauty to be discovered and that the darkness is not limitless.

· · · · ● · ● · · ·

You don't have to hit rock bottom to learn the lesson of letting go. But I've found that those who've been through the darkest moments often understand it more deeply.

They've seen how heavy life can become, how consuming the darkness can feel. And because they've been there, the light—when it finally appears—feels all the more precious.

It's strange how life works that way. Sometimes, you can't fully appreciate the sweetness of a moment until you've tasted bitterness. It's like eating your favorite ice cream after being sick for weeks. The flavors feel richer, the sweetness more profound, because you've been without it.

This reminds me of the old theory of yin and yang—that good and bad, light and dark, are not opposites but rather partners in balance. They sharpen and define one another.

Joy might seem flat without grief. Easy might seem normal without struggle. It's the contrast between the two that gives life its depth, its texture, its meaning.

The hard times don't erase the good ones; they make them shine brighter. And when you've walked through darkness, even the smallest flicker of light feels like a sunrise.

I have come to see life is a roller coaster—not a straight road. Thrilling highs abound when everything seems ideal and full of delight. Then there are those terrible drops when your stomach contracts, and you feel as though you are ceaselessly falling into the future.

But here's what I've learned: both parts matter. The exhilarating climbs wouldn't feel nearly as sweet without the heart-pounding drops. The lows give meaning to the highs, and the fear makes the joy even more profound.

When something difficult or painful happens, I try to remind myself that it's just one part of the ride. It might feel like I'm plunging downward now, but that's not the whole story.

Although this part of the ride is not enjoyable, it prepares me for the next climb. Sometimes, the most unexpected turns lead to the most breathtaking views.

It's hard to see the bigger picture when you're in the middle of the fall, but I hold onto the belief that every drop, every turn, every climb is taking me somewhere meaningful—even if I can't see it yet.

Letting go hasn't just changed how I deal with grief—it's changed how I see everything. Seeing life in vivid color on a large screen feels like I have upgraded from viewing life on an old black-and-white TV.

Every minute seems more alive, every detail sharper. I never noticed before; even the difficult sections have a weird beauty.

I often wish to share this feeling with everyone I meet, like a hidden treasure map leading straight to peace and happiness. But I know it doesn't work that way. Everyone has to find their map and path.

The best I can do is share my story. Perhaps someone out there will hear it and identify a component of themselves in these terms. Perhaps it will provide hope when most needed for them.

When I look back, I am so appreciative of all of it—the good days, the difficult ones, the times of brightness, and the long evenings of darkness. Each one has been a piece of a larger puzzle.

And now, when I look back at that puzzle, I see a picture that isn't perfect but mine. Every edge, every corner, every color tells a story. And even with its imperfections, I love it.

Writing this memoir has been like walking through a landscape of memories and emotions—a journey I didn't fully understand when I first began. It started with Talal, but somewhere along the way, it became about so much more.

It's strange how telling someone else's story can reveal so much about yourself. Through these pages, I've learned that life isn't about avoiding pain but finding meaning in it.

• • • • ● • ● • • •

Some of the toughest events in life teach the most important lessons, like finding a gold coin in a muddy puddle. You have to face the mess, get your hands dirty, and probe deeply to find the buried riches.

For me, the greatest lesson has been about letting go. It wasn't easy—it still isn't. Letting go means surrendering, trusting, and loosening the tight grip I had on my fears, my grief, and my expectations. But once I allowed myself to let go, everything changed. It felt like I had been carrying a heavy backpack my entire life, and I finally set it down.

Now I see how every piece of my story is connected—the good moments, the painful ones, the lessons, and the love. It's all part of one intricate narrative. And Talal's story isn't separate from mine—it's woven into it, a golden thread running through every chapter.

I hope that by sharing this journey, someone out there might find a little light in their darkness. Maybe they'll realize that even the most painful moments can become stepping stones to something meaningful.

As I close this chapter, I feel excited about what's ahead. Life is still unpredictable, still filled with challenges and unknowns. But now, I face it with hope, trust, and a sense of peace I never thought I'd find.

And who knows? Maybe the most beautiful chapters of my story are still waiting to be written.

The Resolution

Finding Peace and Clarity After the Storm

I used to believe that loss was an enormous, terrifying monster that would never go away. But over time, I discovered that loss can be like an old friend who pays occasional visits. Dealing with the sadness of losing Talal was quite difficult at first. I had to be strong and keep moving forward, even when it felt impossible.

Grief doesn't follow a schedule. One moment, I'd be laughing and enjoying myself, and the next, a thought of Talal would tighten my throat and fill my eyes with tears. It sneaks up on you when you least expect it.

Many try to quickly distance themselves from depressing emotions. They wish not to be depressed or cry. I discovered, though, that allowing yourself to experience those feelings is vital. It's like shaking a soda bottle—the pressure has to be released finally. We have the same emotions; we have to let them come out to begin to heal.

I still get sad sometimes when I think about Talal. But now, the sadness isn't as overwhelming as it used to be. It feels more like a gentle ache in my heart. And that's okay—it means I still care.

As the sadness became gentler, I noticed my heart felt more open. I could feel love and happiness again, and grief taught me to appreciate the good things in life even more deeply.

So now I know it's alright to feel sad sometimes. Those feelings might appear suddenly, but they don't last forever. Each time I allow myself to feel them, it's like giving my heart a warm embrace. It helps me remember the good times with Talal and feel grateful for the people I still have in my life.

I was recently at a memorable *Sahur* supper. Among the energetic scenes, I encountered a woman I hadn't seen in over a year. She fixed me closely and asked, "*Dalia, what happened to you? You have transformed. Something distinct exists. Come, come, let us chat.*"

We found a quiet corner away from the noise and sat down. Our conversation stretched over two and a half hours, though it felt like only moments had passed. She was deeply curious and kept asking, "*What happened to you? Tell me about this past year.*"

I began sharing my journey—the lessons I've learned, how I've grown more aware of my thoughts and emotions, and even the book I'm writing. As I spoke about Talal, I initially felt steady and calm. Then, though, a lump developed in my throat without warning, and tears started to flow in my eyes.

Seventy people gathered around us in the packed hall, and for a moment, I considered keeping everything in and disguising my feelings behind a cool smile. I reached for a tissue instead and let the tears run. I continued, my voice trembling but constant. It also tasted excellent. The release was understated, like a weight lifting from my chest. It dawned on me then… something basic yet significant: *feeling sad is okay.*

Grief is not a weakness; it's a visitor arriving and departing on its own schedule. It carries with it pieces of the love we've shared and the memories we hold close.

I've learned that accepting our feelings, even the messy ones, is essential. We don't have to hide or pretend. It's okay to cry, even in a crowded room. Each tear was like a thread stitching together pieces of my broken heart, helping me feel lighter, freer, and more myself.

This experience reminded me that vulnerability is not something to fear. It's part of being human. It's how we heal, grow, and connect with others on a deeper level.

People sometimes feel it's unacceptable to shed tears in front of others. However, I discovered it's okay! We should not treat ourselves angrily if we are depressed or teary-eyed. Everybody has emotions, so it is crucial to treat oneself kindly.

I used to think I had to be perfect all the time. But that only made me feel worse inside. I've learned that accepting myself is far kinder, even in moments of sadness or vulnerability. After all, how can we show kindness to others if we're constantly hard on ourselves?

Many societies, particularly in the Middle East, where I live, hold the conventional wisdom that men and boys shouldn't shed tears. Their upbringing consists in hearing things like, *"You're a man, don't cry!"* Emotions, however, are not limited to one gender; they are part of being human.

If I were a young boy feeling sad in public, I'd remind myself, "It's *okay to cry. It's okay to feel this way.*" I'd picture the little child inside me who needs a warm hug and reassurance.

Carrying sadness without release feels like dragging a heavy backpack everywhere you go. The weight builds up, eventually seeping out as anger, frustration, or exhaustion.

I now know something quite significant: *bravery does not imply suppressing tears. It involves being truthful with yourself, letting those feelings show themselves, and letting yourself really experience them.*

Showing your emotions is natural; it does not make you less of a person or weak. They demonstrate your reality, your compassion, and your vitality. Remember this the next time you start crying—in public or private: your emotions count. Let them flow. You deserve tranquility; others do, too.

When people suppress their sadness, it doesn't disappear—it lingers and transforms into something else. Sometimes, it transforms into anger, resentment, or even physical discomfort.

I watched this happen to Sami, my husband, during a difficult family event. Type 1 diabetes was diagnosed for our second daughter. That stunned us to our very core.

It felt to me like riding an emotional roller coaster—anger, denial, negotiating with God, and finally, depression. Hoping for a miracle, I silently prayed and engaged in impossible bargains with God. Eventually, I began to accept it, but even now, there are nights when tears quietly find their way down my cheeks. *"Why did this happen to her?"* I often wonder, but I've never wished it on anyone else.

Sami's journey through this was different. While I openly expressed my sadness, he retreated inward. He carried his pain like a heavy stone, and I only saw him cry once or twice in those early days.

As a nurse, I'm used to staying calm during medical crises. Sami usually looks to me for cues on how worried he should be. But this time was different—I felt like I was falling apart.

One night, in the middle of my tears, I told him, *"Sami, for the first time, you're stronger than me in something like this."*

At that moment, something shifted. My words seemed to have opened a dam inside of him. Sami collapsed and let the tears run freely, releasing the feelings he had kept so silently. But his anguish changed shape after that night—anger. He wasn't angry at anyone in particular but at the unfairness of it all. He questioned everything: *"Why does science not have a fix for this? Why must genes play such a nasty part? Was I passing this on to her?"*

His armor became anger, a shield from the unvarnished misery he was not ready for. I could see how hard he was trying to stay composed, to protect us from his pain. But I also knew that bottling it up wasn't helping him heal.

I've noticed that many men channel their sadness into anger because they feel less vulnerable and less fragile. But anger isn't a balm for grief; it's a prison.

Strength is about letting oneself feel, even if it means totally collapsing; it is not about keeping everything in. Healing, I have discovered, does not happen in silence. It occurs in those unguarded raw moments when tears let flow, and words are spoken without regard for criticism.

I hope writing this book and sharing our story might help Sami and others understand that holding sadness inside isn't the solution. Feeling sad, angry, or confused when life gets hard is natural. The important thing is to let those feelings out in a way that doesn't hurt anyone, including yourself.

Whether a toddler, an adult, a man, or a woman, everyone has emotions; it's okay to display them. Being brave is about being honest with yourself, letting those feelings come to the surface, and confronting them with bravery rather than covering your grief with a strong face.

A few days ago, I started reflecting on how my family and I dealt with losing Talal. During a conversation with a friend, she said something that struck me: *"Dalia, you never grieved as a family together."* She was right. We didn't.

Traditionally, families get together for three days to grieve, exchange memories, and help one another when someone dies. But I couldn't stand to face anyone when Talal passed away. I withdrew into my grief and cut off even my closest relatives.

Years later, the silence still lingers. We don't talk about Talal. It feels as though mentioning his name might reopen wounds we've worked so hard to conceal. When someone does bring him up, it's usually to say, *"May he rest in peace,"* and then the conversation shifts.

But silence doesn't erase the pain—it just pushes it deeper inside. I see it in my brother Yasser's quiet demeanor and how my aunts (Talal's sisters) lower their eyes when his name is spoken. The weight of unspoken grief hangs heavily in those moments.

After reading this book and feeling the sting of loss, I hope they realize it's okay to talk about Talal. It might hurt at first, like tending to a wound, but it's a necessary step toward healing.

I dream of the day we can gather as a family, open this book together, and share our memories of Talal. Perhaps we'll cry, perhaps we'll laugh, but most importantly, we'll talk.

Healing doesn't always come in grand gestures; sometimes, it begins with a quiet conversation, a shared story, or a single tear.

Two days ago—at the time of writing this chapter—marked twenty years since Talal passed away. I decided to send a message to my family in our group chat, a space we created in 2016 after my grandfather passed away. My aunts often use it to share stories and memories about him.

I wrote, "Today *marks the 20th year since Talal left us, and I miss him every day so much. I think about him all the time. May he rest in peace, be close to God, and watch over us. Hopefully, one day, we'll be reunited with him.*"

Of the forty participants in the group, just three answered. I was immediately overcome with melancholy. Their quiet seemed weighty, like an unresolved question hanging about. But when I stayed with those emotions, I realized—pain rather than apathy kept them silent.

Sometimes, words become impossible when the loss is too profound. Silence turns into a shield to prevent bringing back wounds that never really healed. Unspoken grief, however, digs deeper into the heart and shows itself as tension, headaches, or inexplicable tiredness. It does not go away.

I wish I could sit with my family and tell them, "It's *okay to talk about Talal. It's okay to feel sad. Those tears you're holding back are not weakness; they're love that needs a way out.*"

Grief is heavy when carried alone. But when shared, it becomes lighter and more bearable.

I look forward to a time when speaking about Talal flows naturally—a time when his name brings warmth instead of hesitation. Perhaps one day, we will gather as a family, sharing our laughter and tears, knowing that remembering him is an act of love, not just loss.

Love changes rather than vanishes when someone leaves our life. It becomes the tales we share, the tears we wipe, and the smiles that show up when we go back over them.

Though I live far away in Riyadh, my thoughts frequently return to my family. I wonder whether they also have this subdued ache in their hearts. I wish I could reach across the miles, warmly embrace them, and whisper, *"It's okay to feel. It's okay to remember."*

As I've been on this journey to understand my feelings better, I've learned something really important: it's okay to let go of expectations. That means I don't try to predict how people will react or force outcomes beyond my control.

When I wrote this book, I hoped it would help my family open up about their grief. But I've also learned I can't make them talk about their feelings. Healing can't be rushed—it's like planting a seed. You can water it, give it sunlight, and care for it, but you can't pull on it to make it grow faster.

I've made peace with knowing that my book is worth it if it helps even one person feel seen, understood, or a little less alone. Whenever someone shares how my words have touched them, it feels like sharing my favorite toy with a friend and watching their face light up—it fills my heart with warmth.

The other day, during Ramadan, I had a moment that reminded me of this truth. I was sharing a meal called Sahur with a lady I know. As we talked, she paused, looked at me, and said, *"There's something different about you."*

We continued talking, and she began to share her story. She spoke about her sadness, her anger toward her mom, and how deeply she missed her father, who had passed away. Her voice trembled as she admitted that she couldn't even remember the exact year her father died—maybe it was 2018 or 2019. Her mind had built a protective wall around the memory because it was simply too painful to face.

I was reminded of something strong in that quiet conversation: *healing doesn't follow a straight road, and grief is extremely personal.* Sometimes, all we need is someone ready to listen without judgment, without corrections—just listening.

Then Maria shared a heartbreaking story with me. She was driving in Dubai when her phone rang. It was her mom calling from Ukraine. Her mom's voice was heavy with emotion as she said, *"Maria, pull over to the side of the road."*

Maria did as her mom asked, her hands trembling on the steering wheel. That's when her mom said the words no child ever wants to hear: *"Your father died. We're on our way to bury him right now."*

The world must have stopped for Maria at that moment. Her father was gone, and she hadn't even had a chance to say goodbye. She knew it would be too late even if she got on the next plane.

As Maria told me this story, her voice broke, and tears began to fall. She kept apologizing, saying, *"This is so embarrassing."*

But I stopped her gently and said, *"Maria, it's okay to cry. Let it all out."*

So she did. She wept openly, releasing the grief she had kept bottled up for so long.

When the tears finally slowed, Maria looked at me with red, swollen eyes and whispered, *"I don't know how I'm going to get past this."*

That's when something clicked in my mind. I remembered something special about Maria—her love for painting. She's an incredible artist, pouring her emotions into every brushstroke.

I said softly, *"Maria, you have such a beautiful gift for painting. Maybe you can use that gift to heal. Why don't you paint your father's portrait? Find a photo of him, and let your love and memories guide your brush."*

For the first time since our conversation began, I saw a flicker of hope in Maria's eyes—a small light breaking through the darkness of her grief.

Sometimes, when sadness feels overwhelming, doing something we love—painting, singing, or writing—can become a bridge to healing.

I hope Maria picks up her paintbrush and begins. Maybe, as she carefully sketches the lines of her father's face, she'll feel close to him again. Maybe, in those quiet moments with her canvas, she'll find a little bit of peace.

Talking with Maria made me realize something profound: sharing our feelings is one of the bravest things we can do. When we keep sadness locked inside, it doesn't fade away—it festers. It can show up as anger, exhaustion, or even physical pain. But when we let those feelings out—through talking, crying, or painting—it's like releasing air from an overfilled balloon. The weight lessens, and suddenly, it feels easier to breathe.

One of the hopes I carry with this book is that my words might help someone like Maria find a way to release their sadness. Maybe they'll cry. Maybe they'll talk to a friend. Maybe they'll pick up a paintbrush and pour their feelings onto a canvas. Whatever path they choose, I hope they remember this: It's okay to feel sad. It's okay to let those emotions out.

Painting is a special kind of therapy. Our active brains calm down while we paint. The whirling ideas disappear, leaving just the link between our hearts and the colors on the painting. Maria is a really outstanding artist. She pays almost meditative, nearly perfect attention to detail. I pictured her seated silently, meticulously drawing every wrinkle on her father's face, every glitter in his eyes. I considered how every brushstroke might contain a whisper of connection or recollection.

"Maria," I said softly, *"it's okay if it takes you a long time to finish. Grief isn't something we can rush through. Take your time. Each stroke of the brush is a step forward."*

Healing doesn't follow a calendar. Some days, the canvas might feel too heavy to face. On other days, it might feel like a sanctuary. What matters is showing up, even if it's just for a few minutes at a time.

I hope Maria picks up her paintbrush and begins. And as she carefully brings her father's face to life on that canvas, I hope she feels close to him again. I hope she finds moments of peace in the stillness of her art.

Sometimes, in those quiet periods of creation, we discover a link between our grief and healing.

· · · ● · ● · ● · · ·

Then Maria shared a beautiful story with me. One day, while scrolling through Instagram, she came across a photo of an older man sitting on the ground, feeding swans. He didn't look like her father, but something about how he sat, the peace in his posture, and the kindness in his gaze reminded her of him. Without hesitation, Maria decided to paint this stranger.

When the painting was finished, Maria felt an overwhelming urge to find the man in the photo. She wanted to know his story, share the painting with him, and maybe—just maybe—find some closure for herself.

She contacted the photographer and asked for help. What followed was an unexpected series of connections. Someone promised to tell her if they saw the man again by the swans. Another mentioned they had once dated his granddaughter and could try to reach her.

Eventually, the granddaughter responded. She was curious and asked Maria, *"Why do you want to find my grandfather?"*

Maria explained, *"I painted his portrait and want to give it to him. It feels important."*

She sent the painting along with a heartfelt letter. Later, Maria admitted that she couldn't remember the exact words she had written. *"It was like my heart was writing instead of my mind,"* she said softly.

It was a moment of pure vulnerability, where grief, art, and connection intertwined.

As Maria finished her story, a spark lit up in her eyes. *"Maybe painting my father's portrait could help me, too,"* she said thoughtfully.

I nodded, *"Yes. And you could even write him a letter, just like you did for the man in the photo. Let your heart speak."*

Sometimes, answers do not come from thinking or planning but from being still, listening to our hearts, and allowing ourselves to create.

Healing isn't always loud or grand. Sometimes, it's found in the quiet moments with a paintbrush in hand, a letter being written, or a memory being honored.

Everyone finds their unique ways to heal when they're sad. Some talk about their feelings, while others paint, write, dance, or sit quietly and reflect. There's no single right or wrong way to carry grief—it's deeply personal, and every path is valid.

Maria's story reminded me of my family and how some avoid talking about Talal. They push their grief deep down, hoping it will disappear. But I've learned a valuable truth: sadness doesn't vanish when ignored. It quietly waits until it's ready to surface again.

I hope my family finds ways to remember Talal one day—to celebrate his life and the love we still hold for him. Maybe they'll paint like Maria, write letters, or share stories of his laughter and kindness. However they choose to honor him, I hope they know that it's okay to feel sadness and let those feelings out. Grief is a reflection of love—it's not something to hide or be ashamed of.

Sharing our grief through words, art, or actions lightens the burden. It's like carrying a heavy backpack but with a friend by your side to help you bear the weight.

Helping Maria find her path to healing reminded me why I'm writing this book—to share what I've learned about walking through grief and sadness. If my story helps even one person feel less alone, then every word is worth it.

Grief is like walking through a long, dark tunnel. The only way out is through. You can't skip ahead or turn back. But as you keep moving forward, step by step, you begin to see a faint light in the distance.

Everyone moves through grief differently. Some write in journals, pouring their sadness onto the page and burning the paper as a symbolic release. Others talk to trusted friends, cry in the quiet hours of the night, or create art that captures the love they still carry.

During my journey, I began to notice something beautiful. With time and patience, the heavy weight on my chest began to lift. I could breathe more easily, and the fog started to clear.

I wish I could share this feeling with my family. I wish I could tell them, "If *you allow yourself to feel the sadness, it will eventually make space for love and peace.*"

When I think of Talal, I see his smile so clearly. I remember the light in his eyes and how he made me laugh. Once hidden treasures, these memories have become shining jewels I can visit anytime I want.

Grief isn't about letting go—it's about holding on in a different way.

· • • ● • ● • • ·

Sometimes, the sad feelings come back when we least expect them. And you know what? That's okay. Sadness doesn't follow a schedule, and it doesn't knock politely before entering our hearts. It comes and goes like waves at the beach—rising, falling, then retreating again.

Instead of fighting those feelings or hiding from them, I've learned to let them wash over me. They're not here to drown me; they're here to remind me that love and grief are intertwined.

Grief feels a lot like cleaning out an old, messy closet. At first, it's overwhelming—you don't know where to start. But as you slowly sort through each item, you might stumble upon forgotten treasures: a happy memory, a shared laugh, a twinkle in Talal's eye.

I hope my family can experience this, too. If they allow themselves to sit with their sadness, they might discover hidden joys tucked away in their hearts—moments with Talal that bring a smile, even through tears.

Healing doesn't mean forgetting; feeling better doesn't mean leaving Talal behind. Grief doesn't erase love; it makes room for even more.

When I think of Talal now, I see his smile so clearly. I remember the sparkle in his eyes and the warmth of his laughter. These memories don't hurt anymore—they feel like a soft, cozy blanket wrapped around me on a cold day.

Peace isn't always about grand gestures or perfect moments. Sometimes, it's as simple as a quiet mind. Finding stillness feels almost magical in our fast-paced world, where thoughts race like cars on a busy highway.

Though not in the way most people define it, peace is heaven. It is not only a far-off location with golden light and flowers. Sometimes heaven is a feeling—a tranquility inside your chest, a moment of stillness in a world gone crazy.

If your heart is peaceful and your mind is tranquil, that is bliss, even though you could be standing in the middle of a crowded street or beside a stenchful garbage bin.

And I'll welcome them like an old friend when those sad feelings return—because they always will. I'll let them come, stay for a while, and gently leave again.

· • • ●•●• • ·

Yesterday felt strange. As I sat quietly, a realization hit me—I couldn't stop thinking about the young man who crashed into Talal's car. Though I had not thought about him in years, his face kept showing up in my head.

"*Was my heart trying to communicate something?*" I asked myself. "*Was this a component of my path of recovery?*" Perhaps my mind was nudging me softly to go back over a chapter I hadn't completely closed.

I couldn't even remember his name—Mohammed, perhaps—but I remember his story. He was young, no older than 19 or 21. He was driving on the long road between Riyadh and Khobar while Talal was in the opposite direction. It was Ramadan, and they were both fasting.

The accident happened because the young man fell asleep at the wheel. His car hit a truck and drifted across the highway into Talal's lane. I can't help but feel sadness when I think about those final moments—the fear they both must have felt... the helplessness.

The young man died instantly. Talal, however, lived for a few more moments. And in those moments, it felt so profoundly unfair. Why did Talal have to suffer when the other driver didn't?

But here's the strange part: I was never angry at that young man. Not even once.

My anger had always been directed elsewhere—towards God. I couldn't understand why He would allow something so cruel to happen. Our minds are strange like that; when we can't make sense of tragedy, we search for someone to blame, even if it's God.

But now, sitting with these thoughts, I realize something has shifted within me. I'm not angry anymore. The sharp edge of that emotion has softened into sadness—sadness for two young men whose lives were cut short far too soon.

I wonder if thinking about the young man now means I'm finally ready to forgive—not just him, but everything. The accident. The circumstances. Myself.

Healing isn't linear. Sometimes, it feels like our minds are sorting through a box of scattered puzzle pieces, trying to fit them into something that makes sense.

Maybe revisiting this memory will teach me something important: *that grief isn't about holding on to blame but finding peace.*

• • • ● • ● • • •

This experience let me realize something very important: *healing goes beyond only improving your own self. It also involves knowing and forgiving others, especially in cases when it seems unfeasible.* Years later, I never would have imagined thinking about the other driver—wondering about his family, experiencing grief for them, and understanding how tragedy affects every person engaged.

Growing up really means, I think, realizing that life is seldom black and white. Sometimes, events occur because life is erratic and delicate rather than because someone is to blame.

After Talal's funeral, something extraordinary happened. The family of the young man who caused the accident came to visit my grandfather. They wanted to apologize and ask for forgiveness. I wasn't there, but I remember hearing about it later.

The young man was his family's only son. He had seven sisters, and his mother had waited so long to have him. When I consider her loss, my chest gets constricted. The weight of her loss—the dreams she had for him, the happiness he offered her, and the agony of losing him so quickly—is just unimaginable.

Still, the fact that my grandfather forgave them stayed with me the most.

My grandfather adored Talal. He was the youngest grandchild, the light of my grandfather's eyes. And yet, in that moment of grief, my grandfather extended grace and forgiveness to the family.

That day, without saying a word, my grandfather taught me one of the most powerful lessons of my life: forgiveness isn't about letting someone else off the hook—it's about freeing yourself from the burden of anger and blame.

I started to think about forgiveness differently. I thought about forgiving the young man who caused the accident. I thought about forgiving God, even though that was one of the hardest things I've ever had to do.

But do you know what was even harder? Forgiving myself.

I had to forgive myself for not answering Talal's phone call before the accident. For not getting to say goodbye. For holding onto my sadness for so long without allowing myself to heal.

Forgiveness isn't easy—it's like cleaning out a messy, cluttered closet in your heart. It's hard labor; occasionally, you come across something that makes you cry. Once the labor is done, though, your heart seems lighter. You find it simpler to breathe. And perhaps at such flashpoints of clarity, you might at last begin to heal.

• • • ● • ● • • •

I've realized something important: *grief isn't just about crying or missing someone. It's about learning to forgive—the person who caused the loss, God, and most importantly, yourself. It's one of the hardest lessons and the most healing.*

Reflecting on this journey, I see how far I've come. I'm not the same person I was when Talal passed away. The person I was back then felt fragile, shattered into pieces. But slowly, I've stitched myself back together, piece by piece.

This path has taught me about love—not just my love for Talal, but the love I've learned to show myself. It's taught me about forgiveness—not as an act of letting someone off the hook, but as a way of freeing myself from the chains of anger and regret.

It feels like I've been climbing a long, steep mountain. And now, standing here at the peak, I can see the world differently. The air feels clearer, and the view is brighter. There's a warmth in my chest—a golden glow of peace and forgiveness that radiates outward.

This ability to carry love where anger once lived feels almost like a superpower. It's not flashy or loud; it's quiet, steady, and deeply rooted.

But here's something else I've learned: healing isn't just about feeling better after a tragedy. For many people, healing only begins after something breaks them open. It's like they've been asleep, and suddenly, life pours a bucket of ice-cold water over their heads.

That moment—the wake-up call—is when they begin to ask questions, search for answers, and look for a way forward. Often, they find themselves on a path like mine.

Grief is a teacher. It's not gentle, and it's not easy, but it's powerful. And if we allow it, grief can guide us—not just to acceptance but to transformation.

That's why grief—and any challenging experience—feels so powerful. It's like being strapped into a rollercoaster that loops, dips, and twists unexpectedly. Sometimes, it feels thrilling; other times, terrifying; and occasionally, exhausting.

But here's something I've learned: it's not only the big, tragic moments that shape us. Even the small, frustrating things—the little setbacks, the daily inconveniences—are part of this same emotional journey.

The real magic happens when we listen to the sound of silence. It's like turning down a loud TV's volume. The planet seems suddenly to be quieter, crisper, and more vivid. It's almost like donning magic glasses, allowing us to perceive beauty in the most minute details—the way sunshine dances across leaves, the sound of laughter far away, or the warmth of a sincere smile.

And something else shifts, too. Our behavior changes when our perspective of the world does. We answer with love, patience, and compassion rather than wrath, anxiety, or annoyance. It's not because we're working harder—it's because something inside of us has softened.

It is like holding a heart gradually and steadily blazing from warm, golden illumination. This illumination comes from neither the need to prove anything nor fear or rivalry. It emanates from a pure love source.

And here's the amazing fact: *others notice this transformation in us.*

Yesterday, a woman I know looked at me curiously and said, *"What happened to you? You look so different!"* She studied me, trying to pinpoint what had changed—as if maybe I'd gotten a new haircut or was wearing new clothes. But the truth is, it wasn't something visible on the outside. The change had happened deep inside—somewhere in my heart and soul.

This change feels like a quiet, golden energy radiating outward. It doesn't shout for attention, but those around me feel it. And when you carry that kind of light inside you, it attracts warmth and kindness back into your life—like a gentle, endless ripple spreading across still water.

This transformation feels like carrying a quiet, radiant energy—a kind of warmth that others can sense without fully understanding why. They might not know the reason, but they're drawn to it, like moths to a mild light. With this energy, it's as if the world starts to respond differently. Doors open, opportunities appear, and moments of connection seem to happen effortlessly. Some people might even call it *magic*.

It feels like standing in a golden ray of sunlight, basking in its warmth, and realizing that this light isn't external—it's coming from within. And when you carry this light, it naturally spills over to those around you.

But getting to this place wasn't easy. It was like climbing a steep, rocky mountain during a stormy night. There were moments when I felt like turning back, moments when every step felt impossible. But I kept going—one small, determined step at a time.

Standing at the peak, I can look back and see how far I've come. The climb wasn't easy, but every challenge shaped me into who I am today.

I've learned that feeling sad, angry, or afraid isn't something to be ashamed of. These emotions are natural—they're part of being human. But I've also learned something equally important: we don't have to let these feelings take over our lives.

We can feel them, honor them, and then release them when the time is right, like letting go of a balloon and watching it drift gently into the sky.

When I wake up these days, the world feels different. Colors seem brighter, small moments feel more meaningful, and gratitude fills even the quietest corners of my day.

I notice things I used to overlook—the way sunlight filters through leaves, the sound of a bird's song, the kindness in a stranger's smile. And I'm grateful—not just for the joyful moments but also for the painful ones because they helped me grow.

Sharing my story through this book feels like planting seeds in a garden I may never see fully bloom. But I hope that someone—somewhere—will read these words and feel a spark of hope.

Even in the darkest times, there's light. Sometimes, it's hidden beneath layers of hurt, anger, or fear. But it's always there, waiting patiently for us to find it again.

And when we do, it feels like coming home.

• • • ● • ● • • •

Reflecting on my life, I realize that healing isn't just something I've experienced—it's become my life's purpose. Healing feels like a vast umbrella, shading everything I do. Whether through nursing, writing, or mentoring, each path has been a thread woven into this larger purpose.

My journey as a nurse was one of the earliest ways I learned about healing—not just for patients but for myself. Writing this book has been another powerful way to heal. In sharing my story, I hope to extend a hand to others walking their difficult paths.

But before I could help anyone else, I had to heal myself. That was one of the hardest lessons to learn—I needed to address my sadness, anger, and fear before I could guide others.

In Saudi Arabia, I've been working as a coach and mentor. This is my second year, and it's a role I've come to cherish deeply. Coaching allows me to show up as my authentic self—to share my feelings and experiences openly, without hiding behind a mask.

It's incredible to see how vulnerability creates safety. When I share my truth, it encourages others to share theirs. We're holding hands on this journey, creating a chain of healing and trust.

When I'm with my mentees, I often imagine myself as a warm, cozy blanket wrapped around them. It's a safe space where nothing bad can happen, and they can let their guard down. In this safe bubble, stories flow freely, like water rushing from an open tap.

At 42 years old, I've carried many stories with me. I used to hold onto them with shame or fear, but not anymore. I've shed the heavy backpack of self-judgment, and now I carry those stories lightly, with love and acceptance.

Lately, I've been drawn to the idea of life coaching. It feels like a natural next step—a way to expand my ability to help others. Then, I heard about holistic wellness coaching, and something clicked.

Holistic coaching isn't about fixing one broken part of a person—it's about seeing them as a complex puzzle. It's about recognizing how every piece fits together to create something beautiful. It reminds me of painting a rainbow—each color adds unique beauty to the bigger picture.

This approach aligns perfectly with everything I've learned as a nurse, mentor, and human being.

Ultimately, everyone needs this—to be seen not just for their struggles or pain but as a whole person with layers, colors, and stories that make them who they are.

And I'm ready to keep learning, growing, and healing to help others do the same.

If I Had One More Moment

Dear Talal,

I've carried the weight of your absence in ways I never expected. I thought I had time. Twice, I thought I had time. And twice, saying goodbye slipped through my hands. But if you're here now—if there's even a moment to speak what was left unsaid—I need you to know...

I never stopped thinking about you. Never stopped wishing I could have just one more moment.

I don't know if you knew how much I loved you. I hope you did. But just in case, I'll say it now, louder than I ever could before.

You are not forgotten.

You are not just a memory, not just a missing piece—I carry you with me, always.

And if I could go back, I'd tell you I'm sorry for the moments I wasn't there. That I never wanted you to leave this world.

But maybe love is bigger than the moments we miss. Maybe it lingers, reaches beyond time, beyond words, beyond everything we think separates us.

And if that's true... then you never really left, did you?

And maybe that's enough. Maybe that's what you already know.

But if there's more in my heart, I'll always say it. Even if you can't physically be here to hear it, I'll say it. I know you already know. But maybe I need to say it to set myself free.

I love you.

Epilogue

G rief is not a single moment—it's a lifelong companion. It doesn't disappear; it transforms. Over time, it becomes softer, quieter, and less consuming. But it never fully leaves.

When I began writing this book, I thought I was preserving Talal's memory. But somewhere along the way, I realized it was about so much more. It was about allowing myself to feel every emotion, sit with the discomfort, and surrender to the healing process.

Talal's story isn't one of tragedy—it's one of love. His kindness, warmth, and quiet wisdom continue to guide me even now. I hope this book reflects his light and helps others navigate their path through grief.

To anyone holding this book, I want you to know that healing isn't linear or quick. It is raw, messy, and quite intimate. Still, it's also quite lovely. Every tear you shed, every memory you go back over, and every quiet moment of acceptance moves you toward peace.

Closing this book, I carry Talal with me—not as a weight but as a lighthouse. My words, actions, and the still times when I most sense his presence reflect his love life.

Though it has not broken me, grief has changed me. And in its wake, I have found something priceless: love, meaning, and hope can all abound in life, even after death.

I appreciate you traveling this road with me. May your bridge across loss be found by bravery, love, and an open heart, then crossed.

Acknowledgements

I would like to express my deepest love and gratitude to all those who have made the book possible and complete.

First and foremost, I would like to thank my family and friends. Reopening the wounds was not easy on us, but it has contributed greatly to my healing, and for that, I am forever grateful. Their unwavering support, understanding, and encouragement have been a constant source of motivation.

I am also very grateful to my parents (Yasime and Osama) for their unconditional love and support.

I would like to thank the publisher, H.J. Chammas from Authority Publishing, for his trust and belief in this book. He has been a critical part of my healing, pushing me and giving me the space to be vulnerable. His guidance has been immensely helpful.

Lastly, to all the readers who relate to the book in some way, I hope you can find some peace in reading it.

This book would not have been possible without the collective efforts of everyone around me.

Dalia

About the author

Dalia is a healer, nurse, and mentor who has dedicated her life to supporting others during their most vulnerable moments. Her first book was inspired by her own journey through grief—a transformative experience that led her to help others find healing and hope.

In 2022, Dalia experienced a profound inner awakening when she left her job of 17 years to embark on her doctorate journey. During this period, she spent a year attending retreats to rediscover herself and gain clarity on her purpose. These transformative experiences deepened her connection to her calling and shaped the heartfelt guidance she offers in her writing.

Drawing from her personal journey and professional expertise, Dalia weaves reflections of resilience, self-discovery, and hope into her work. This book stands as a testament to her belief in the power of healing, love, and the human spirit to find light even in the darkest times.